W9-AVA-487

Professional Sports

EXAMINING POP CULTURE

JAMES D. TORR, Book Editor

Daniel Leone, President
Bonnie Szumski, Publisher
Scott Barbour, Managing Editor

GREENHAVEN
PRESS®

THOMSON

GALE

San Diego • Detroit • New York • San Francisco • Cleveland
New Haven, Conn. • Waterville, Maine • London • Munich

For more information, contact
Greenhaven Press
27500 Drake Rd.
Farmington Hills, MI 48331-3535
Or you can visit our Internet site at http://www.gale.com

LIBRARY OF CONGRESS CATALOGING-IN-PUBLICATION DATA

Professional sports / James D. Torr, book editor.
    p. cm.—(Examining pop culture)
Includes bibliographical references and index.
ISBN 0-7377-1588-X (pbk. : alk. paper) —
ISBN 0-7377-1587-1 (lib. bdg. : alk. paper)
    1. Professional sports—Social aspects—United States. 2. Popular culture—United States. I. Torr, James D., 1974– . II. Examining pop culture.
GV583 .P758 2003
796.04'4—dc21
                                      2002192519

CONTENTS

as skateboarding have gained unprecedented national exposure and popularity.

Chapter 2: Sports Reflect American Values

Chapter 3: Women and Minorities in Professional Sports

Chapter 4: Professional Sports as Show Business and Big Business

Chapter 5: America's Obsession with Sports and Sports Stars

FOREWORD

POPULAR CULTURE IS THE COMMON SET OF ARTS, entertainments, customs, beliefs, and values shared by large segments of society. Russel B. Nye, one of the founders of the study of popular culture, wrote that "not until the appearance of mass society in the eighteenth century could popular culture, as one now uses the term, be said to exist." According to Nye, the Industrial Revolution and the rise of democracy in the eighteenth and nineteenth centuries led to increased urbanization and the emergence of a powerful middle class. In nineteenth-century Europe and North America, these trends created audiences for the popular arts that were larger, more concentrated, and more well off than at any point in history. As a result, more people shared a common culture than ever before.

The technological advancements of the twentieth century vastly accelerated the spread of popular culture. With each new advance in mass communication—motion pictures, radio, television, and the Internet—popular culture has become an increasingly pervasive aspect of everyday life.

Popular entertainment—in the form of movies, television, theater, music recordings and concerts, books, magazines, sporting events, video games, restaurants, casinos, theme parks, and other attractions—is one very recognizable aspect of popular culture. In his 1999 book *The Entertainment Economy: How Mega-Media Forces Are Transforming Our Lives*, Michael J. Wolf argues that entertainment is becoming the dominant feature of American society: "In choosing where we buy French fries, how we relate to political candidates, what airline we want to fly, what pajamas we choose for our kids, and which mall we want to buy them in, entertainment is increasingly influencing every one of those choices. . . . Multiply that by the billions of choices that, collectively, all of us make each day and you have a portrait of a society in which entertainment is one of its leading institutions."

It is partly this pervasive quality of popular culture that makes it worthy of study. James Combs, the author of *Polpop: Politics and Popular Culture in America*, explains that examining

7

popular culture is important because it can shape people's attitudes and beliefs:

> Popular culture is so much a part of our lives that we cannot
> deny its developmental powers. . . . Like formal education or
> family rearing, popular culture is part of our "learning envi-
> ronment.". . . Though our pop culture education is infor-
> mal—we usually do not attend to pop culture for its "educa-
> tional" value—it nevertheless provides us with information
> and images upon which we develop our opinions and atti-
> tudes. We would not be what we are, nor would our society
> be quite the same, without the impact of popular culture.

Examining popular culture is also important because popular movies, music, fads, and the like often reflect popular opinions and attitudes. Christopher D. Geist and Jack Nachbar explain in *The Popular Culture Reader*, "the popular arts provide a gauge by which we can learn what Americans are thinking, their fears, fantasies, dreams, and dominant mythologies. The popular arts reflect the values of the multitude."

This two-way relationship between popular culture and society is evident in many modern discussions of popular culture. Does the glorification of guns by many rap artists, for example, merely reflect the realities of inner-city life, or does it also contribute to the problem of gun violence? Such questions also arise in discussions of the popular culture of the past. Did the Vietnam protest music of the late 1960s and early 1970s, for instance, simply reflect popular antiwar sentiments, or did it help turn public opinion against the war? Examining such questions is an important part of understanding history.

Greenhaven Press's *Examining Pop Culture* series provides students with the resources to begin exploring these questions. Each volume in the series focuses on a particular aspect of popular culture, with topics as varied as popular culture itself. Books in the series may focus on a particular genre, such as *Rap and Hip Hop*, while others may cover a specific medium, such as *Computers and the Internet*. Volumes such as *Body Piercing and Tattoos* have their focus on recent trends in popular culture, while titles like *Americans' Views About War* have a broader historical scope.

In each volume, an introductory essay provides a general

overview of the topic. The selections that follow offer a survey of critical thought about the subject. The readings in *Americans' Views About War*, for example, are arranged chronologically: Essays explore how popular films, songs, television programs, and even comic books both reflected and shaped public opinion about American wars from World War I through Vietnam. The essays in *Violence in Film and Television*, on the other hand, take a more varied approach: Some provide historical background, while others examine specific genres of violent film, such as horror, and still others discuss the current controversy surrounding the issue.

Each book in the series contains a comprehensive index to help readers quickly locate material of interest. Perhaps most importantly, each volume has an annotated bibliography to aid interested students in conducting further research on the topic. In today's culture, what is "popular" changes rapidly from year to year and even month to month. Those who study popular culture must constantly struggle to keep up. The volumes in Greenhaven's *Examining Pop Culture* series are intended to introduce readers to the major themes and issues associated with each topic, so they can begin examining for themselves what impact popular culture has on their own lives.

INTRODUCTION

"IT HAS BEEN REPORTED OVER AND OVER AGAIN by sociologists and psychologists that sports have taken on a central role in the daily lives of millions of Americans, sometimes even exceeding politics, community service, religion, or family in importance," writes sports historian Richard O. Davies. For example, more Americans watched the January 1999 Super Bowl (133 million) than had elected President Bill Clinton in 1998 (48 million). The national obsession with pro sports is partly documented in financial terms. Writing in 1997, economist Wilbert M. Leonard II noted,

> The professional sports industry has burgeoned into one of the most significant mass-entertainment industries in American society. In 1995 . . . the 109 franchises in professional baseball, basketball, football, and hockey were estimated to be worth over $11 billion. . . . The gross national sports product, GNSP, today is around $85 billion and is predicted to be in the $120 billion range by the year 2000. This would make it the eighth largest industry in North America!

A December 1999 study in the *Sports Business Journal* estimated the size of the American sports industry to be $213 billion.

The emergence of sports as such a major social force is a relatively recent phenomenon. Modern sports fans, as Davies puts it, "would scarcely recognize the American sports scene during the years immediately following World War II. Professional sports had a modest, even provincial quality about them. Only professional baseball and boxing attracted substantial national attention." Major League Baseball teams were confined to the Northeast and upper Midwest, since they traveled only by train. The National Football League (NFL) had been formed in 1922 but paled in comparison to baseball and college football in popularity. The National Basketball Association (NBA) was formed from the merger of two competing leagues in 1950, but like football it took a distinct backseat to the college game. The National Hockey League (NHL) had been founded in Canada in 1917 but was slow to capture American audiences.

The Postwar Boom

The incredible success of pro sports in the second half of the twentieth century was due primarily to two changes in U.S. society. First, the economic boom that followed World War II created a larger, more affluent middle class. As Davies explains, "Economic growth produced not only substantially higher levels of discretionary income, but also more leisure time." Pro sports were just one of many aspects of popular culture—along with entertainment staples such as movies and music—to flourish in America's new consumer culture.

Television was the second factor that propelled professional sports to national significance. By 1960, television sets were in almost 90 percent of American households. Sporting events, which had traditionally been local affairs that fans paid to attend, now became national events that millions of viewers could enjoy for free. This had several effects on pro sports. First, individual sports teams gained much wider fan bases, since a far larger number of people were able to watch the games. Second, some sports—notably boxing and minor league baseball—were devastated by drop-offs in attendance, as fans stayed home to watch televised events instead. Third, the games themselves were changed in various ways to better fit a television format. For example, "TV timeouts" were introduced in basketball.

But by far the greatest effect that television had on the four major sports leagues—Major League Baseball, the NFL, the NBA, and the NHL—was to make them much more profitable than ever before. As regular-season games and national championship events such as the World Series and the Super Bowl drew (and continue to draw) increasingly larger TV audiences, television networks were able to demand increasingly higher rates from advertisers. Thirty seconds of advertising time during the 2001 Super Bowl, for example, cost an estimated $2 million. The TV networks, in turn, have to pay the major pro sports leagues enormous sums for broadcasting rights. In 1980, for example, Major League Baseball earned $80 million from local and network television. In 1990, this figure increased to $612 million, and in 1996, it was $706 million. In 1998, CBS, Fox, ABC, and ESPN paid the NFL a combined $17.6 billion for eight years of broadcasting rights.

America's Obsession

Many critics have charged that the very success of pro sports threatens to alienate some fans as the cost of supporting their favorite team escalates. Broadcasting fees typically account for less than half an individual team's revenue in these leagues; ticket sales, concession stand sales, stadium advertising, and licensed merchandise provide the rest. From 1991 to 2000, ticket prices for the four major pro sports increased 80 percent—four times faster than the Consumer Price Index, which gauges the average rate of inflation. While some critics argue that the leagues are exploiting fans in order to increase owners' profits and players' salaries, economists point out that the leagues are charging what the free market will bear. In other words, attending pro sports games may cost what it does simply because fans are willing to pay so much.

The financial cost of being a sports fan may not be the only downside of Americans' obsession with pro sports. John R. Gerdy, author of *Sports: The All-American Addiction*, believes that this obsession is fundamentally harmful to the national culture: "We have become addicted to sport; it is our society's opiate. . . . Like a drug addiction, being a sports fan offers little of long-term substance or meaning. It allows us to escape our problems and ignore the issues we face."

A Mirror of Society

However, while pro sports may be a form of escapism for individual fans, pro sports can, like other seemingly trivial aspects of popular culture, provide meaningful insights about society as a whole. "The close observer of contemporary American sports can learn much about the national condition. Sports have become a microcosm of national life," writes Davies. In *A Brief History of American Sports*, authors Elliot J. Gorn and Warren Goldstein write that "a critical study of sports history teaches Americans about who we have been and who we would like to be, about worlds we have lost and opportunities we have gained, about how we have worked and played." A 1999 *Newsweek* retrospective on professional sports in the twentieth century noted that "sports increasingly became a prism through which America views some of the time's most complex issues—race, gender, drugs, unions, spousal abuse, and AIDS."

For example, pro sports have served as an important arena for civil rights. Jackie Robinson's breaking Major League Baseball's color barrier in 1947 is now recognized as one of the seminal events in the early civil rights movement. Thirty years later, tennis champion Billie Jean King's defeat of self-proclaimed male chauvinist Bobby Riggs became one of the most celebrated events of the feminist movement. These and countless other triumphs demonstrate how pro sports reflect one of America's most cherished values: equality of opportunity. Yet a close examination of pro sports also shows how pervasive discrimination still is. As Gorn and Goldstein point out,

> Sports are still dominated by men, and they have remained a source of male privilege and power, of masculine language, metaphor, and memory. Moreover, sports that officially banned black players half a century ago now routinely offer them million-dollar contracts. Those same sports, however, generally keep their doors to management and ownership closed to minorities. So it is fair to say that sports have given voice to the hopes of particular groups for equality, and dramatized their efforts to attain it; but the history of sports also contains overwhelming evidence of the persistence of inequality.

In addition to reflecting American society, pro sports often represent American culture to the rest of the world. As *Newsweek's* retrospective on twentieth-century pro sports notes, "Sports may be America's most successful export to the world. Michael Jordan is arguably the most famous man on the planet. . . . Our most visible symbol has, over the 20th century, evolved from the Stars and Stripes to Coke to the Nike Swoosh. Whatever the world thinks of us, it loves our games."

Like the rest of popular culture, the sports world is characterized by change. To maintain their enormous popularity, the major sports leagues and the individual teams that compose them are constantly adapting to new technologies and changing public tastes. The formation of new professional leagues such as the Women's National Basketball Association and the Women's United Soccer League may signal a new era for women's sports, and the emergence of extreme sports in the early 1990s may signal a new emphasis on individuality in U.S. culture.

Examining Pop Culture: Professional Sports is intended as a guide to show how sports have historically served as a mirror of society, and how they continue to reflect major trends and issues within American culture. This volume highlights some of the major themes in professional sports, while encouraging readers to further explore the connections between professional sports and the society that so passionately supports them.

1

EXAMINING *POP* CULTURE

The Rise of Professional Sports in America

The Rise of Professional Sports in the Twentieth Century

David Halberstam

David Halberstam is a prolific journalist and the author of numerous books on both political topics and sports, including *Playing for Keeps: Michael Jordan and the World He Made.* In the following selection, he traces the rise of professional sports in America, paying particular attention to how this rise reflects American cultural and economic progress. The popularity of professional baseball in the early decades of the twentieth century, for example, was an outgrowth of the prosperity that followed the Industrial Revolution. When Jackie Robinson became the first black player in Major League Baseball in 1947, it foreshadowed the civil rights struggles of the 1950s. The popularity of the Super Bowl in the 1960s accompanied the nation's embrace of its role as a superpower, and the many controversies surrounding Muhammad Ali's career reflected the political tensions of the 1970s. Halberstam concludes with a discussion of Michael Jordan and the future of pro sports.

RARELY HAD THE BEGINNING OF A CENTURY IN one nation seemed so distant from the end of the same century. In January 1900 the [United States] was barely a genera-

■

tion removed from a bitter and exceedingly violent civil war, yet from that war were the beginnings of American power, dynamism and industrialism first fashioned.

But that was yet to come. If the Civil War had been fought to end slavery, then there was in the Reconstruction era, as the true political price of reunion emerged, a resurgence of racism, slavery replaced by legal racism, and fierce continued suppression of the children of slaves. If, in Lincoln's phrase, a house divided against itself cannot stand, then America as the century began was neither a house divided nor a house unified. In the new century, one of the great struggles played out would be that of black Americans struggling for full citizenship. And no arena would showcase this battle in a series of stunning and often bitterly divisive increments, or reflect the true talents of black America more clearly, than the world of sports. . . .

America was, of course, almost without knowing it, a favored nation. The quality and energy and passion of its immigrant citizens and the part they were to play in the successes of the coming century were not to be underestimated: They were to become inventors, scientists, workers, farmers and exceptional citizens. . . .

This explosion of affluence and power and confidence connected directly, it would turn out, to the world of sports; more, the world of sports would serve as an almost ideal window through which to watch the profound changes taking place elsewhere in the society. Was the country more confident, more affluent, and did its citizens have more leisure time? Then they would show it by becoming more addicted to their games.

No one signified the coming of power quite like Babe Ruth. He changed the very nature of sports. He was five years old when the century began (or at least he so believed, since it was also possible that he was four years old). Because his deeds were so awesome, particularly when measured against the existing dimensions of what passed for power, his name was almost immediately turned into an adjective. Long drives, more than half a century after he played his last game, are said to be Ruthian. He was the perfect figure about whom to create a vast assortment of myths and legends, some of them true, some of them not, though it meant little if they were true or not, because the ones which had been made up seemed just as true as those which could more readily be documented. . . .

He brought drama to everything he did. He was not just a great athlete, he was a show, fun even when he struck out. He became a phenomenon. Ordinary people longed to read about him. The outrages he committed socially were the outrages of the common man, the ordinary American catapulted to an elite world by his athletic success, but unspoiled in his heart. After he had signed for $80,000, a salary greater than that of President Herbert Hoover, and a reporter questioned him about it, he had said, "Why not? I had a better year than he did." When he met Marshall Foch, the commander of the French forces during World War I, he had said, "I suppose you were in the war."

If Ruth was the most egalitarian of sports heroes, then this was the most democratic of lands, the nation where mass production—and a new kind of economic democracy that went with it—was born. It was not by chance that the new century was perfectly designed for America, and indeed was often known as the American Century. That was a partial misnomer. In truth, it was the Oil Century, as the Japanese intellectual Naohiro Amaya called it, for it was a century in which gas-driven machines would replace coal-driven machines, with an explosive increase in productivity. In the oil century productivity flowered; it could generate products enough for everyone—not just for the handful of rich. The oil culture because of the nature of the fuel created vastly more wealth, a wealth so great that it was shared by ordinary people. And of all the industrialized nations poised for the start of a new era, America, with its rich indigenous oil deposits, was uniquely well-positioned for the new age.

In the oil culture, because oil produced so much more in the way of goods, the workers became prosperous, too. The oil century produced, it would soon become clear, workers who would become consumers; and the more they consumed, the more they created work for others. It was the dawning of a culture in which ordinary people achieved not merely middle-class status, but an elemental social dignity which had in the past been reserved for a tiny number of people. This was an American invention—a nation with something new, a mass middle class. The citizens in this new society gained dignity, confidence, leisure time and, in time, disposable income. That alone was to have a profound effect on the rise and the obsession with sports in the century ahead. . . .

[In the twentieth] century America became a vastly more dynamic, vastly less class-dominated, infinitely more open society than competing nations. Its people were busy; they were on the move, driving all the time now, it seemed, prosperous, and ever more confident. Its love of sports became a parallel force. The more confident and affluent Americans were, the more they became sports nuts. In addition, other inventions were taking place which would not only bind America together more as a nation, but make sports an ever more important part of the fabric of the society.

It was not just the games themselves that were about to change and become more important. It was the delivery system—the coming of modern broadcasting, first radio, then network television, and then satellite television—which was going to change the way Americans felt about sports; for the new, more modern delivery system was about to make the games more accessible (and thus more important) and make the athletes themselves infinitely more famous, and soon, infinitely wealthier. In the beginning, there was radio. It would help usher in what became known as the Golden Age of Sport. In 1923 the Yankees defeated the Giants in the World Series in six games. Ruth hit three home runs, was walked constantly and scored eight times. It was a noteworthy series, not the least of all because it was the first time the World Series was broadcast across the country on radio. . . .

On a vast, sprawling land mass where the connection of ordinary people to each other had often been tenuous, big-time sports, broadcast to the entire nation at one time, giving the nation shared icons, was to prove immensely important. It was not just a shared moment of entertainment, though that was critical in the rise of the popularity of sports, but it was to be an important part of the connecting tissue of the society, arguably more important in a country so large where the population was so ethnically diverse—and new—than it might have been in a smaller country with one dominating strain of ethnicity. Sports in some way united America and bound Americans to each other as other aspects of national life did not—it offered a common thread, and in time a common obsession. Americans who did not know each other could find community and commonality by talking of their mutual sports heroes. . . .

Americans by means of radio could [by 1930] monitor their sports heroes as never before. Events in the world of sports seemed to be ever more important and hold the attention of the public that much more. The resulting popularity of sports was amazing, as was the resilience of its appeal throughout the Depression. On the eve of World War II, baseball seemed to be poised at a level of almost unique preeminence. The 1941 season was a historic one: Joe DiMaggio hit in 56 consecutive games and Ted Williams hit .406. Soon both were in the service, and baseball, like other sports, went on essentially a four-year vacation.

If World War I had been the first act of America's emergence as a world power, World War II would be the defining act. . . .

For the war changed the balance of power in the world with a certain finality: In Europe the old powers had been bled white by two wars; America, by contrast, had been brought kicking and screaming to the zenith of its power. No bombs had fallen on America; its losses—roughly 350,000 men on two fronts—were slight in comparison with other nations.

All of these factors had given the nation a startling boost in affluence, household by household, and equally important, a critical increase in personal confidence. Not only had America as a nation played a decisive part in the war, not only had it been, in contrast to most wars, considered a good war, but millions of Americans, whose professional careers might in an earlier part of the century have been proscribed by class, had left their small towns, had learned that they could lead men, and now had a chance to continue their careers through the G.I. Bill. If one of the things which distinguished America from the old world was its concept of social fluidity—the fact that in only one generation ordinary citizens could rise significantly above the level attained by their parents—then nothing made that concept more muscular than the G.I. Bill.

In the postwar era America had to face the domestic consequences of its own wartime rhetoric. For the war had generated its own powerful propaganda, that of the democracies taking on two totalitarian powers, Germany and Japan, and in the case of Germany a racist, genocidal nation. But there were important domestic consequences to that. If America was the driving force of a new, more democratic world, then it was still a nation divided racially, not just in the South, where feudal laws imposed state-sanctioned legal and political racism, but in the North as well, its major professional sports events still lily white. In the courts a large number of cases trying to end the doctrine of separate but equal were working their way to the Supreme Court. But it would be the world of sports that became the most important postwar laboratory of racial change and where black Americans finally got their first true chance at showing their real talents. That their sports were segregated was singularly unjust, and no one knew this better than the professional baseball players themselves. For they often barnstormed with black players from the Negro League after the season, and they knew exactly how good the black ballplayers were, that only racial prejudice prevented them from playing.

Jackie Robinson, whose terrible responsibility it was to be the first, the man in the test tube, his abilities and conduct to be scrutinized by an entire nation—was nothing less than history's man. He was a superb athlete, strong, quick, and wildly competitive. He had been a four-sport star at UCLA before he played professional baseball, and he could probably have played professionally in three major sports. Before he entered the service in World War II, though professional basketball and football were still quite embryonic in the West, he played with semi-pro teams in both.

He brought with him a rare on-field and off-field intelligence, and exceptional mental discipline and toughness of mind, an ability to restrain himself despite extreme provocation (and control his hair-trigger temper). He resisted, as he promised he would, the temptation to lash back for a long time despite the constant taunts of fans and opposing players. "Mr. Rickey, what do you want?" he had asked the Brooklyn Dodger boss at their fateful first meeting. "Do you want a player with guts enough to fight back?" "I want a player," Rickey had answered memorably, "with guts enough not to fight back." He might rage inside, but he remained true to the challenge offered him by Rickey. Throughout his career,

Robinson remained aware that the spotlight was always on him, and that the challenge to excel on field and behave with dignity off it was singular in his case. Few Americans were ever subjected to such relentless scrutiny in so public a manner; it is doubtful if any of his fellow citizens ever endured such relentless pressure with such sustained excellence. . . .

It was a great experiment, and it took place in 1947, seven years before *Brown v. Board of Education*. In a way, what Jackie Robinson did, performing in the most public arena in America, was every bit as important as that Supreme Court decision in 1954. His arrival in the big leagues had been the ultimate test on something that most Americans prided themselves on—the fairness of their country, that in this country the playing field was somehow supposed to be fair. In a way it was an experiment which put America itself at a crossroads between two powerful competing national impulses, one impulse reflecting the special darkness of racial prejudice and historic meanness of spirit which had begun with slavery, the other the impulse of idealism and optimism, that a true democracy offered the children of all American citizens a chance to exhibit their full talents and rise to their rightful place. What he was contesting was the worst myths of the past, for in the particular cruelty of the time, America had not merely barred blacks from its professional leagues, it had said it was barring them because they were unworthy. Yes, the rationale went in those days, they could run fast, but they lacked guts and heart, and they would fold in the late innings in big games, and, of course, by the way, they were lazy—everybody knew that.

By midseason the argument was over. Robinson was a great player—clearly on his way to becoming rookie of the year. He had brought life and speed and intensity to an otherwise more passive Dodger team. He was an American samurai, the baseball player as warrior, and the other Dodgers became more like him—they were with his arrival much more a warrior team that fought you all the time than they had ever been in the past, and they would remain that way for the duration of his career. As a player no one was more explosive. Pitchers in particular feared him once he was on the base paths because of his explosive initial burst of speed. Years later, the Yankees pitcher Vic Raschi, talking about how he had lost a 1–0 game in the 1949 World

Series by giving up a hit to Gil Hodges, said that it was Robinson, bluffing a dash from third toward home, who had beaten him. "I had just never seen anything like him before, a human being who could go from a standing stop to full speed in one step. He did something to me that almost never happened. He broke my concentration, and I paid more attention to him than to Hodges. He beat me more than Hodges."

If Robinson's stunning success against the myths of the past marked the first great breakthrough of the postwar era, then the second one was driven by technological change. It was the coming of network television and it started as a true national phenomenon roughly a decade after the end of the war. It inaugurated nothing less than another golden age in sports. For in truth the world of sports as the postwar era started actually had two golden ages ahead, both of them driven by technological breakthroughs, the first one wrought by the coming of network television which dramatically boosted football as a sport, especially the professional game, and the second some 25 years later with the coming of satellite transmission, which created the world of cable television and aided all sports, most particularly basketball. . . .

Before the coming of television, professional football was, in comparison to baseball, virtually a minor league; it was a very good game, indeed a connoisseur's game, played by immensely talented athletes before passionate, diehard fans, but it had somehow never quite broken out of its rather narrow place in the sports spectrum. Radio revealed neither the talent nor the fury with which it was played. To the degree that ordinary sports fans committed their time to football on fall weekends—it was on Saturday when they could pick up a Notre Dame or Michigan game on the radio, not Sunday.

Sunday became in the new televised age the day which was set aside in the fall for American males. It introduced the pro game to a vast new audience, and the pro game began to enter the consciousness of average sports fans as never before. Very quickly in the mid to late Fifties, as the country was wired nationally for television, pro football went on a dizzying rise to a point where it began to rival professional baseball as the national sport. In those days not that many people owned sets, and many young American males would agree to meet at a neighborhood bar to watch and eat and drink. The sense of a sport on the rise was obvious—and nowhere was that more obvious than in New York, where the football Giants began to become something new in pro football ranks, media celebrities. Football stars like Frank Gifford, movie-star handsome, were doing commercials (for very little money, mind you), and being welcomed as never before in bars like Toots Shors, where baseball players, fighters and jockeys had held forth. The game was coming of age.

With the coming of network television professional football became a truly national game, with a national constituency. A fan did not have to live in Baltimore to be a Unitas or a Colts fan, or for that matter to live in New York to root for the Giants defense led by middle linebacker Sam Huff. Millions of sports fans who cared nothing about Pittsburgh, had never been to the University of Louisville, and had no intention of ever visiting Baltimore turned on their sets on Sunday to watch the daring exploits of a young quarterback from Pittsburgh who had gone to the University of Louisville and now played for the Baltimore Colts. The camera, it turned out, was quite dazzled by Johnny Unitas, the least likely, it would seem, of American media heroes. . . .

Unlike [Joe] Namath (and [Muhammad] Ali), who came after him and understood intuitively that in the new sports world created by television, it was always both sport and show, he always thought it was merely sport. His values had been set in that earlier age. Yet Unitas became the first superstar of the new age, the signature player of an old sport amplified by a new and loving medium, the perfect working-class hero for a sport just beginning to leave its working-class roots behind. . . .

In 1958, in what was later called the greatest game ever played, Unitas led the Colts to victory in overtime in the championship game against the Giants. He did it with two spectacular long drives, one at the end of regulation, the other in the sudden-death overtime. It was a signature game. . . .

Professional football ascended in popularity like a comet. In 1960, a second league was founded, and its star quarterback Joe Namath, coveted by both leagues because he had star quality, signed for $400,000. In just a few years more, the leagues merged, and played the defining event of America the Superpower in the Super Century, the Super Bowl.

The rise of the nation in the postwar era to this pinnacle was constantly contentious. Isolationist before the war, it was now a leading international power. On the way the debate over race had become ever more barbed. In the early Fifties there had been a powerful challenge to the existing Jim Crow rules in the South. By the late Sixties, the existing laws had fallen, but the mood of American blacks was changing, and there were constant signs of the powerful alienation just under the surface. The black power movement began to flourish in the late Sixties—its slogan was black is beautiful, and in northern cities, the old religious ties which had been so important to black life in the South had begun to wither. A new movement, that of black Muslims, seemingly threatening to whites—its principal leaders spoke of white people as devils—had taken root among the deeply embittered blacks of the nation's northern cities.

That meant that a young man named Cassius Clay, who rose to fame as a heavyweight boxer, was to become at once the most dazzling, and the most controversial athlete of his era, a symbol of all the powerful societal forces let loose in the Sixties.

He also in some way understood that television had changed the nature of sports, and no one, it would turn out, was a better entertainer; no one knew better how to hype his own fights. He was, he understood, as much actor as he was fighter, and he was exceptionally skilled at casting not just himself, but his opponents to his specifications. He himself, he liked to proclaim, was beautiful. His opponents were not. Sonny Liston, the most threatening of men until Ali completely defanged him, was too ugly, he boasted, to be the champ. . . .

In the end he was a marvel, a figure not only of sports but, like Jackie Robinson, though in a different way, of history itself. The day after he became heavyweight champion, he had announced that he was a Muslim and that his name was Muhammad Ali. A few years later, because of the war in Vietnam, he refused induction into the army, citing his religious principles. So it was that he lost his crown—and the ability to fight—for more than three years.

Politically, time worked on his side: By the Seventies, the Muslims were perceived to be less menacing. Dissident, and alienated, certainly, as blacks who lived in the poorer parts of

America's cities might well feel alienated and dissident, but not that threatening. As for the war in Vietnam, that became something of a badge of honor, that Ali had dissented, and acted upon his dissent; he, it turned out, had paid the price for others on a war which was something of a scar on the national conscience.

In time he regained his crown. Older now, several critical years wasted, he returned, his conscience having been served, to fight better than ever, to demonstrate in his fight with [George] Foreman in Zaire and in three wondrous battles with Joe Frazier his true greatness.

His was a sobering challenge to America's self-image at a volatile and emotional time. He, the most marginally educated young man, barely able to get through high school (he got his high school degree only because the officials at his school realized that he was going to be the school's most famous product, and that it would shame the school rather than Clay if he did not graduate), had turned out to be right about a war about which the most brilliant national security advisers who had gathered around the President—including the Dean of Harvard college, the former head of the Ford Motor Company, and the former head of the Rockefeller Foundation—had turned out to be wrong. That was sobering, a reminder that America at the height of its affluence and power in this century had lost sight of what its true meaning and purpose was. The arrogance of power, the head of the Senate Foreign Relations Committee, Senator William Fulbright, called it. Ali would never have been able to come up with a phrase like that—instead he simply said, "I ain't got no quarrel with the Vietcong." He had acted upon conscience; the advisers, even when they were later burdened by doubt as the war went forward, had not. He had paid the price for his actions when he was young; they, the architects of this disaster, would pay it when they were older. That, for a nation which in its increasing power had become too prideful, too sure of its value and its rectitude, was a sobering lesson. No wonder, then, by the Nineties he had become something of a beloved national figure.

The success of Ali, the quality of his singular struggles, so much of it political, makes a sharp contrast with that of the final surpassing athlete of this era, Michael Jordan. The two had much in common: Both were supremely talented, both were black, both with their looks, their talent, and their style transcended their sports, appealing to millions of Americans who nominally had little interest in either boxing or basketball.

There the comparisons end, and the Americas they performed for differ. They are produced by different Americas: Ali by an America which seemingly closed off all of its benefits to a young talented black man from the South, other than the most brutal, primitive road to fame, boxing; Jordan, born in a time which made him a beneficiary of all the modern civil rights struggles. He was born in 1963, a year before Ali as Clay won the heavyweight title. He went to integrated public schools and was able to go on and star at North Carolina, a school which only recently had been closed to black undergraduates and which at the time of his birth still had not fielded a black basketball player on its team. His parents were comfortably middle class, his father by dint of victories in another hard-won battle—that of blacks in the American military. At Carolina Michael received the kind of great education and exceptional coaching that had been denied black athletes in the past.

Jordan was the most charismatic athlete of his era, and he was the best big-game, fourth-quarter player of a generation. He helped carry a team which often in other ways seemed somewhat ordinary to six world championships. He was the perfect figure for the American communications and entertainment society as the century came to a close, the first great athletic superstar of the wired world, arguably the most famous person on the planet. In [one of his last seasons] as a player, he earned some $78 million, $33 million in salary and $45 million in endorsements. It seemed only proper that as the century ended, he was engaged in serious negotiations to buy a large part of an NBA team.

He was a new world prince, graceful, beautiful, but a warrior or samurai nonetheless, and easily recognizable to the rest of the world as such. He arrived, unlike those before him, such as Robinson and [Willie] Mays and [Hank] Aaron, in a nation which had begun finally to realize that it was not a white nation, and as much as any other American he was proof that America, in some way, despite all its ethnic and racial divisions, was moving toward the beginning of a universal culture.

He gave the nation nothing less than a new concept of beauty. Not surprisingly, his comfort zone was singularly high. He was gifted, he worked hard, and was beautiful in a nation which was now willing to accept a more complicated definition of beauty. America, after some 30 years of racial turbulence, was delighted to have a gifted young black man who seemed to be smiling back at it. If he endorsed sneakers, millions of Americans bought them, and in time he sold hamburgers and soft drinks and underwear and sunglasses and batteries and a telephone company.

As the century ended, he was known everywhere in the world, for the sport he played, basketball, was easily understandable, and traveled smoothly across borders in a way that American football and baseball did not. For in the new age of inexpensive satellites, America exported not its autos or its machine tools, but its culture—its music, its sports, and finally, the informality of its lifestyle. And Jordan was the most luminescent figure of the new world, his deeds the easiest to comprehend and admire.

It had been, all in all, an astonishing century for America. No other country had ever changed so much in so short a time—rising to a position as a monopoly superpower, gaining steadily in power, affluence, and innate self-confidence. In this period much of the change, and the interior struggle, could be witnessed in the world of sports. It was not so much a metaphor for the society as a window on it—the tension, the conflicts, and the constant progress had often taken place first (and been witnessed more widely) in the world of sports. That was true, whether it was the rise of black athletes or the greater independence of the athletes themselves as they enjoyed greater personal freedom. Throughout the century, sports had served as a remarkable reflection of the strengths and weaknesses of the nation—its diversity, its hungers, its excesses, its rank commercialism. But above all the fact that the athletes always seemed to get bigger and stronger and faster, and the games themselves better.

Baseball in American History

Jules Tygiel

The following article is adapted from Jules Tygiel's introduction to *Baseball as America: Seeing Ourselves Through Our National Game*, a companion volume to the National Baseball Hall of Fame's traveling exhibit of the same name. In it, Tygiel puts the history of professional baseball into the broader context of American history, discussing how baseball served as a symbol of national unification after the Civil War, a symbol of economic and technological progress in the early twentieth century, and a symbol of social progress in the 1940s and 1950s. He also discusses how the rise of mass media increased the game's popularity. Baseball's rich history, Tygiel concludes, has earned it its reputation as the national pastime.

Jules Tygiel is a professor of history at San Francisco State University and the author of *Baseball's Great Experiment: Jackie Robinson and His Legacy* and *Past Time: Baseball as History*.

THE GAME HAD FEW ADHERENTS PRIOR TO 1855, when it became a virtual overnight sensation, first in the New York metropolitan area, and then throughout the nation.

Simultaneously, baseball entered the American cultural mainstream. In 1858, J.R. Blodgett of Buffalo, New York, published "The Base Ball Polka," the first known baseball song. This ditty was followed within a decade by songs like "Home Run Quick Step," "The Base Ball Quadrille," "The Base Ball

■

Fever," and "Catch It on the Fly."

Popular lithographers Currier and Ives demonstrated the extent to which baseball had penetrated the American consciousness in a remarkable print depicting the results of the 1860 presidential election. The illustration—entitled "The National Game. Three 'Outs' and One 'Run'"—featured Abraham Lincoln and his three defeated opponents dressed as baseball players and wielding bats. Each of the men discussed the outcome of the election using baseball terms. One wondered "why we should strike 'foul' and be 'put out.'" Another spoke of putting a "short stop" to Lincoln's career. Lincoln, himself, explains that to emerge victorious one must "have a good bat" and strike a "fair ball" to make a "clean score" and a "home run." Currier and Ives felt confident that its national clientele would understand the baseball imagery and be familiar with the language of the game. Within a few years, baseball terminology had already invaded and begun to transform the American vernacular.

During the 1860s, amidst Civil War and Reconstruction, baseball further cemented its hold on the nation. The first baseball book designed for fans, *Beadle's Dime Base-Ball Player*, appeared in 1860. Eight years later, William Everett wrote *Changing Base*, the first in a long line of fictional baseball works for children. In 1866, *Frank Leslie's Illustrated Newspaper* described the first baseball table game, Parlor Base-Ball, created by former pitcher Francis C. Sebring.

In the aftermath of the war, baseball, an increasingly popular spectator sport, became a symbol of reunification. In 1868, an estimated 200,000 people attended baseball games. The following year the Cincinnati Red Stockings, the first professional team, toured the nation, attracting 179,000 fans and capping their travels with a western excursion aboard the recently completed transcontinental railroad. The primary ambassadors of the national pastime traveling on the foremost symbol of a new America captured the essence of the modern era.

By the time the National League emerged in 1876, many of the rituals of the game had already become commonplace. Thanks to the pioneering efforts of sportswriter Henry Chadwick, fans could follow the daily progress of their favorite teams and players through intricate box scores concisely summarizing the previous day's play and ingenious statistics, like batting average, designed to measure each athlete's prowess and productivity. Fans could purchase scorecards that allowed them to keep a meticulous record of each player's performance as they watched the game.

As baseball expanded its influence in the late 19th century and became the nation's most popular participatory and spectator sport, the game also materialized in a wide variety of cultural venues. The Philadelphia Centennial Exposition of 1876 displayed artist Thomas Eakins's watercolor, "Baseball Players Practicing," in its celebratory exhibition. Cards depicting famous baseball players began to appear as premiums accompanying packs of cigarettes in the 1880s. Old Judge Cigarettes produced a set of large cabinet cards, with players posed in studio photographs for display in tobacco shops—a forerunner of the more widespread use of athletes in advertising. Table and card games brought baseball into the parlor. Lawton's Patent Base Ball Playing Cards, introduced in 1884, used a 36-card deck to simulate the play on the field. Four years later, J.H. Bowen created a mechanical bank, equipped with a pitcher who flipped a coin placed in his hand into the catcher's chest, where it would drop into a box, as an idle batter stood by. Bowen's original model, dubbed "The Darktown Battery," featured African Americans as the athletes. Despite, or perhaps because of, its inherent racism, this version and its many successors became popular keepsakes.

Baseball often came to embody and encapsulate each new wave of American progress. Mark Twain called it "the very symbol, the outward and visible expression of the drive and push and rush and struggle of the raging, tearing, booming 19th century." One of the first demonstrations of the efficacy of Thomas Edison's electric lightbulb in 1880 involved a baseball game played at night at a seaside resort in Massachusetts. Electricity also allowed fans to experience games nearly instantaneously. Beginning in 1894, the Compton Electrical System appeared in many cities. The new system took play-by-play results from the telegraph and relayed them to a 10-by-10-foot display depicting a baseball diamond. The opposing lineups were listed on either side of the diamond, and lights indicated the batter, the count, and the base runners. During World Series contests in the early 20th century, these scoreboards attracted tens of thousands of spectators in arenas, central urban intersections, and town squares throughout the nation.

Edison, among the nation's foremost inventors, also turned to baseball as the focus of one of his first moving pictures, *The Ball Game*, in 1898. Indeed, as the movies matured, baseball, both on and off the field, often provided a prime subject. The adventures of fans sneaking off from work to see a ball game figured prominently in a pair of early two-reel films: *How the Office Boy Saw the Ball Game* (1906) and *How Jones Saw the Baseball Game* (1907). Efforts by gamblers to bribe an honest player provided the basis for *His Last Game* (1909).

Aspiring newsreel companies also quickly latched on to baseball action as a source for appealing footage. In 1908, the California-based Essanay Company filmed the World Series, editing the highlights into brief films and distributing them to local theaters. The first true newsreels surfaced in American theaters in 1911. By the end of the teens, sports events, especially baseball, accounted for as much as 25 percent of all newsreel footage.

In 1915, the same year that D. W. Griffith popularized the feature-length film with *Birth of a Nation*, the first full-fledged baseball movie, *Right Off the Bat*, made its debut. *Right Off the Bat* starred "Turkey" Mike Donlin, a former National League standout playing himself in a narrative loosely based on his career. Giants manager John McGraw had a cameo role. The success of the movie led other ballplayers to try acting. Ty Cobb headlined *Somewhere in Georgia* (1916), portraying a bank clerk with baseball skills who wins his way onto the Detroit Tigers. Babe Ruth portrayed a country bumpkin who whittled his own bats in *Headin' Home* (1920). "There is no reason for John Barrymore or any other thespian to become agitated about the matter," commented one critic about the Babe's acting skills.

Radio, Television, and the Internet

In the 1920s, baseball became a major vehicle for introducing radio to the American public. Pittsburgh radio station KDKA went on the air in November 1920. In its first summer on the air, the station's innovative broadcaster, Harold Arlin, covered a Pirates game live from Forbes Field. That fall, WJZ in Newark, New Jersey, stationed a correspondent at the World

Series in New York. The reporter telephoned play-by-play to an announcer in Newark, who recreated the game over the air, inaugurating a venerable radio tradition. In 1922, Westinghouse used the prospect of listening to the World Series as a lure for potential radio customers, advertising the opportunity for New York fans to hear sportswriter Grantland Rice broadcast the games from the Polo Grounds. Stores that sold radios erected loudspeakers for the occasion, attracting crowds of the devoted and the curious. The result was what the *New York Herald Tribune* called "the greatest audience ever assembled to listen to one man."

The following year, announcer Graham McNamee took over at the microphone. His dramatic renderings drove home the power and romance of radio. McNamee became the voice of the World Series for the remainder of the decade, offering millions of people throughout the nation their first radio experience. McNamee brought "something vital into the living room," recalled future announcer Red Barber. McNamee would pause to let his listeners hear the cheers and jeers of the crowd, and, as one sportswriter noted, "these little inserts of realism transplanted the atmosphere of the diamond to every nook and corner of the United States."

As early as 1924, individual teams and local radio stations began to experiment with regular game programming. In the late 1920s, five Chicago stations carried the Cubs home games. Teams in St. Louis, Cleveland, Detroit, Cincinnati, and Boston also offered regular transmissions. A new type of celebrity, the baseball broadcaster, took hold in many cities. Fred Hoey in Boston became, in the words of a fan, "a regional giant. Fred was Boston baseball." In Detroit, Ty Tyson "made you feel like (Charlie) Gehringer, (Mickey) Cochrane and (Goose) Goslin were right next door."

Many feared that the availability of games in one's own home would keep fans from attending the games. More astute observers, however, recognized that radio would broaden the audience for baseball. The 1920s combination of regional radio, improved roads, and automobiles, noted John Sheridan, had expanded the radius of a team's market from five miles to 200 miles, bringing more fans to the ballpark. In midwestern towns, crowds would gather around loudspeakers to follow the progress of games played in nearby cities. In the 1930s and 1940s, national radio networks sprang up to carry games across the country. The Mutual Broadcasting System presented a *Game of the Day* every afternoon except Sundays. Gordon McClendon's Liberty Broadcasting Network flourished in the south and southwest, with a game of the day, game of the night, and Sunday games as well.

Baseball shared the same symbiotic relationship with early television. Television manufacturers offered "World Series specials" to entice people to purchase sets. People who could not afford televisions could watch through the windows of appliance stores or in bars and restaurants. As early as 1947, an estimated 3,000 New York City bars had installed televisions, "the best thing to happen to the neighborhood bar since the free lunch." In 1951, live telecasts became available in most parts of the nation. Many people experienced their first glimpse of television watching the Yankees and Giants in the 1951 World Series, sending television sales soaring.

Once again, many feared that the new technology would decimate baseball attendance. "Radio stimulates interest. Television satisfies it," pronounced Brooklyn Dodger executive Branch Rickey. "TV Must Go Or Baseball Will," warned an article in *Baseball Magazine*. Television, by offering a broader variety of sporting events, did ultimately weaken the unique bond that had long existed between baseball and the American public. But, in the long run, it inevitably enhanced the baseball experience, giving people the opportunity to see more games, in more intimate detail, than ever before.

In more recent times, baseball helped to usher in the computer age. Few bodies of data offered the opportunities to demonstrate the capabilities of the computer as readily as did the universe of baseball statistics amassed since the age of Henry Chadwick. In 1959, researchers perfecting mammoth mainframe computers constructed models of play based on thousands of theoretical games. General Electric showed off a new computer model by having it analyze American League batting. In 1969, the *Macmillan Baseball Encyclopedia*, a landmark computer compilation of baseball history, also became the first book typeset entirely by computer.

In the 1980s and 1990s, millions of Americans took ad-

vantage of personal computers and the Internet to revolution-
ize the use of baseball statistics, manage Rotisserie leagues,
and follow the progress of major and minor league teams in
minute detail. Online gamecasts, instantaneously displaying a
diamond and lineups, recreated the electronic scoreboards of
an earlier age, though now the scoreboards materialized in
one's home, rather than a public square, and offered a variety
of statistics far beyond anything that Chadwick might have en-
visioned.

The technological innovations of each era influenced the
manner in which Americans experienced baseball. Similarly,
baseball mirrored the broader political, social, and economic
changes of American history. The emerging professional game
quickly became a beacon of opportunity for players and entrepreneurs alike. The formation of the National League and rival baseball alliances in the late 19th century reflected the ra-
tionalizing impulses of American businesses in the industrial
era. Like other enterprises, baseball faced labor difficulties, resulting in the formation of a National Brotherhood of Base
Ball Players and a short-lived Players' League in 1890. Baseball developed its own peculiar forms of exploitation—the re-
serve clause and, later, the farm system—to regulate its labor
supply. For many years a relatively limited regional cartel
based in the northeast and midwest, Major League Baseball in
the post–World War II era followed the nation's population
and business trends. Transplanting existing franchises and creating new ones in California and the west, the south and
southwest, and expanding into Canada, this produced a truly
national and international pastime.

Baseball also replicated the nation's racial practices. The
game held a broad appeal for both white and black Americans,
but from the earliest years of play, most leagues and associations excluded African Americans. By the late 19th century,
parallel baseball worlds, separate but unequal, had crystallized.
Jim Crow in baseball, however, more than in any other endeavor, visibly challenged the tenets of segregation and discrimination. Negro league superstars like Satchel Paige and
Josh Gibson clearly did not lack the talent to compete against
whites. Nor did interracial contests regularly played on the
boundaries of organized baseball—on the barnstorming circuit,

in the winter leagues, in semiprofessional tournaments—support the notion that interracial play meant interracial conflict.

When the turmoil of the Depression and World War II began to challenge the prevailing racial consensus, baseball stepped to the forefront as a vehicle of change. In 1945, Brooklyn Dodgers president Branch Rickey recruited Jackie Robinson to defy the color line. Robinson's dramatic and convincing triumph produced a modern American legend and a blueprint for social revolution. The success of African Americans in baseball offered one of the nation's most compelling arguments for integration, making it a significant precursor of the civil rights triumphs to follow.

Robinson's achievement had such a profound impact precisely because baseball had such an intense hold on the American psyche. As Thomas Wolfe has written, baseball is "not merely 'the great national game,' but really the part of the whole weather of our lives, of the thing that is our own, of the whole fabric, the million memories of America."

The National Pastime

No other common activity resonated so regularly and intensely in American life as the national pastime. Played virtually every day over a six-month span and tracked religiously in the mass media, baseball offered its partisans a steady diet of entertainment, drama, and controversy. Americans routinely interspersed their language with baseball metaphors. Unexpected occurrences came from "out of left field." People confounded others by "throwing them a curve." Prodigious feats were described as "Ruthian."

In a "fireside chat" broadcast on the radio in May 1933, President Franklin D. Roosevelt presented his hopes for his new administration to the American people in a language they would readily understand. "I have no expectation of making a hit every time I come to bat," explained Roosevelt. "What I seek is the highest possible batting average, not only for myself, but for my team." In the last days of his life, Roosevelt confessed: "I feel like a baseball team going into the ninth inning with only eight men left to play."

A host of rituals that tied baseball to the American way also accumulated over the decades. Annual Opening Day festivities were celebrated as rites of spring in major and minor league cities across the land, laden with pomp, circumstance, and panache. Season openers brought forth brass bands, parades, and aerial displays. Public officials threw out the first pitch. Some cities declared holidays for municipal employees and schoolchildren. The national anthem, sung before each game, became ineradicably entwined with the national pastime. The All-Star Game and World Series became engrained American spectacles, with red, white, and blue bunting draped along the field boxes in prominent view.

The development of a rich mythology also linked baseball to American patriotism. A blue-ribbon panel of statesmen, baseball leaders, and military veterans, determined to demonstrate the powers of American ingenuity, decreed in 1908 that baseball had not evolved from earlier games like rounders, but that it had sprung, Athena-like, from the fertile mind of Gen. Abner Doubleday, in Cooperstown, New York, in 1839. The pairing of baseball and Doubleday, a Civil War hero, tied America's national game to its most sacrosanct conflict, making baseball's version of the immaculate conception a part of the nation's folklore. That Doubleday had not been present in Cooperstown at the time and had never mentioned his inspiration did not deter the myth-makers from their appointed round. Nor did it prevent the location of a shrine to the game, the National Baseball Hall of Fame and Museum in Cooperstown, the site of Doubleday's alleged invention. . . .

For many, a journey to remote Cooperstown has become a treasured, ardently anticipated pilgrimage. The plaques honoring the game's greatest athletes; the bats, gloves, and balls used at fabled moments in baseball history; and the variegated assortment of odd relics and mementos that mark the intersection of the sport with American life and culture hold an overpowering allure for those who cherish the game. The National Baseball Hall of Fame and Museum encompasses America's intense relationship with baseball—the patriotism, freedom, rituals, opportunities, popular culture, innovations, and mythology. It reminds us at every turn of why, across the broad historic sweep of American experience, baseball maintains its hold on our imagination and reality and remains, above all other activities and institutions, our enduring national pastime.

Pro Football and the Rise of Sports Television

Richard O. Davies

As with many aspects of popular culture, professional sports did not obtain a truly national audience until the advent of mass media, particularly television. In the following selection from his book *America's Obsession: Sports and Society Since 1945,* University of Missouri history professor Richard O. Davies explains how television led to the ascendancy of the National Football League as one of the most popular and profitable sports leagues in the United States. The lucrative relationship established between the NFL and the national television networks set the precedent for how other sports leagues would be financed, and ABC's innovative presentation of *Monday Night Football* and its *Wide World of Sports* program set new standards for sports coverage and reporting. Davies also notes that television has impacted the games themselves, as professional football, baseball, basketball, tennis, and golf all made rule changes to enhance TV revenues.

IT IS AGREED BY MOST STUDENTS OF TELEVISION sports that December 28, 1958, signals the day when sports television arrived as a major force in American life. On that day professional football took a quantum leap forward toward

■

its envied position as the most popular of all American sports when the Baltimore Colts staged a thrilling drive to tie the vaunted New York Giants in the championship game of the NFL with a field goal on the final play of regulation time. In the ensuing sudden death overtime period, while a national NBC television audience of 30 million viewers watched in suspense, quarterback Johnny Unitas calmly led the Colts down field in a classic thirteen-play drive that was capped by a short run for the winning touchdown by fullback Alan Ameche, giving the Colts a 23-17 victory. More than three decades later, many fans still believe it to be the greatest football game ever played. Perhaps, but it undoubtedly was sports drama at its best. Almost overnight professional football had gained millions of fans—including the leaders of the New York City advertising and broadcasting professions. In the wake of this exciting championship game, professional football grew rapidly in stature and popularity. . . .

[In 1959] the NFL faced the difficult problem of selecting new leadership following the death of longtime commissioner Bert Bell. In mid-January of 1960 the owners of the twelve NFL teams sequestered themselves for several days in the Kenilworth Hotel in Miami to pick a new commissioner. This meeting, which came close to failure because of an inability to reach a consensus, now stands out as the league's defining moment. For several days none of the dozen or so candidates failed to gain the necessary eight votes. *Sports Illustrated* reported that the mood at the deadlocked meeting was one of "stalemate and despair." The owners finally turned in near exhaustion, and some suggested, near desperation to an individual who had initially received only scant attention—the relatively inexperienced and untested thirty-three-year-old general manager of the Los Angeles Rams.

The owners apparently made the compromise selection of Alvin "Pete" Rozelle for all the wrong reasons, but in retrospect the decision seems to have been one of almost divine inspiration. When Rozelle was named the new commissioner on January 26 the NFL had existed for thirty-nine seasons, most of them played before small and indifferent crowds. During that time the league had undergone more than sixty major changes in franchise ownership or team location. Now that it had finally captured the attention of the nation with the thrilling 1958 championship game, it faced the threat of a rival league, whose rules promised a more wide open and exciting brand of football. Although a healthy growth in attendance during the 1950s provided reason for optimism, the future of the NFL was anything but assured.

Bert Bell's leadership since 1946 had enabled the league to grow slowly but steadily; he had brought to the league the confidence that derived from increased stability and occasional profits. But as late as 1952 one team had declared bankruptcy, and as Rozelle assumed office few owners had any realistic dreams of ever turning a substantial profit. The NFL, soon to become an incredible money machine thanks to television, still remained a small-time operation in every sense of the word. The winning members of the Baltimore Colts in that epochal game of 1958 had each received the wondrous sum of $1,500; most player salaries remained well below $20,000, and the value of most franchises hovered around the $1 million level. When Bell died, league offices occupied a few rooms in the back of a small branch bank in suburban Philadelphia. For several years Bell had actually operated the league out of his kitchen! He had, however, enabled the league to withstand the challenge of the All-America Football Conference, ultimately absorbing three of that upstart league's most lucrative franchises in 1950 (Baltimore, San Francisco, and Cleveland), and he had maintained the integrity of the game. But most important, unlike the leaders of baseball, Bell had protected the league from the potential ravages of unrestricted television.

Rozelle's expertise was not in football but in public relations. He had begun his professional career as a public relations staffer for the Los Angeles Rams, moving up to the position of general manager at the tender age of twenty-seven. On football matters he largely deferred to his coaches, concentrating instead on increasing the Rams' income by hyping ticket sales and marketing team memorabilia—beer mugs, T-shirts, sun visors, and the like. But most important, Rozelle had become intimately familiar with the arcane world of television in the aggressive Los Angeles market. It was Rozelle's mastery of the unique business of television that propelled the NFL to a level of power, prestige, and riches that league owners could not have imagined in 1960. Significantly, one of Rozelle's very first decisions was to move NFL headquarters to the nation's media capital, New York City.

It is among the greatest of ironies that Rozelle produced an enormous capitalist bonanza by imposing on the league the essential truths of socialism. Recognizing that the future of the league depended on maintaining the competitiveness of each of the league's teams—"parity" he called it—Rozelle convinced the owners of teams in the major media markets that it was essential to divide all television revenues equally. In Green Bay, the smallest city in the league, the impact of revenue sharing made it possible for that team to remain competitive with teams located in the biggest of media markets; in 1956 the Packers had received just $35,000 from the sale of its TV rights. Having gotten begrudging approval for his plan from such football barons as George Halas of the Chicago Bears, Wellington Mara of the New York Giants, and Dan Reeves of the Rams, who stood to lose the most, Rozelle then spent the summer of 1961 lobbying the U.S. Congress for legislation exempting the plan from federal antitrust prosecution. Congress complied with the Sports Antitrust Broadcast Act, which permitted professional leagues to pool revenues and to sell their television rights as a single entity.

Thus properly armed, Rozelle orchestrated an elaborate plan that placed the three networks under intense pressure from viewers, advertisers, and, especially, their local station affiliates to secure the new television rights for the 1964–65 season. He made certain that the network decision makers fully understood the rapidly growing popularity of the game as he announced the rules for what would become a highly publicized bidding process. Rozelle shrewdly created a scenario placing the three networks in an intense, highly publicized competition with each other; ABC recognized an opportunity to gain credibility as a major network, while NBC and CBS perceived that their prestige was at stake. When Rozelle opened the sealed envelopes the size of the bids astounded even the most seasoned of reporters assembled at NFL headquarters. Rozelle shuffled the three envelopes, opening them at random. He first opened the NBC bid, and he produced gasps of shock when he announced it to be $10.4 million for *each* year! The league's total TV revenue for 1963, in comparison, had totaled just $4.6 million. Rozelle next opened the bid from upstart ABC—it eclipsed NBC's by nearly $3 million! Rozelle recalled, "I thought, based on rumors, that we might get over ten million bucks." But after he had announced ABC's blockbuster, Rozelle found his mind spinning. "My God, the ABC bid was beyond any of my dreams. Even figuring the wildest sort of thing they might do . . . I never thought it'd go as high as $12,000,000." As he opened the CBS bid, Rozelle recalled he was in a state of near shock: "I figured the CBS bid had to be anticlimactic. . . . So I opened their bid kind of lackadaisically. The thing was two pages long—all that fine print. The number itself was sitting way down toward the bottom on the second page. I looked at it, and . . . Goiinnnnnnngggggggg! 'Good God,' I thought, its for $14,100,000 a year!"

It was, by far, the biggest contract in the history of sports. Euphoria swept through the league. When Rozelle called the chair of the NFL television committee, Art Modell of the Cleveland Browns, to report the good news, the conversation went something like this: "Art, Art. CBS got it for fourteen million." A disappointed Modell responded, "We-e-e-ll it could be worse. I did expect a little better, but hell, Pete, seven million a year isn't half bad. We can make it." The ecstatic Rozelle retorted: "Art—Art—Fourteen million a year. Twenty-eight million for two years." After a long pause, Modell replied, "Pete, you've got to quit drinking at breakfast."

This seemingly amazing breakthrough proved to be only the beginning. In future years the staggering figure of $14 million would seem like a bargain basement price. Those who commanded the boardrooms of network television had become aware that sports—properly produced—could generate high viewer ratings, which in turn produced increased advertising revenue. Early in the 1960s the creative Roone Arledge at ABC Sports had discovered an essential fact that had escaped everyone else: viewers in large numbers could be lured into watching sports on television even if they were not much interested in a particular event *if* the program itself was entertaining. Arledge's genius as head of ABC Sports stemmed from his basic premise that he should furnish viewers with entertainment, not merely sports.

When ABC launched its coverage of NCAA football in 1960, Arledge provided viewers with the sounds and excitement of the game unlike anything they had experienced before—picking up crowd noise and the collisions on the field with special microphones, weaving shots of spectators, cheerleaders, and excited coaches into the coverage of the game itself. He instructed announcers like Keith Jackson to present the game in a format that appealed to the casual fan. ABC became known in the business for its "honey shots," pictures of pretty coeds in the stands, dancing cheerleaders, or scantily clad baton twirlers. Color technology made the show much more attractive even to those indifferent to football. Dedicated football fans, however, were enthralled with the introduction of such innovations as the instant replay, slow-motion recreations of important plays, and the many new viewing angles provided by the nine cameras Arledge placed around the stadium. He provided coverage of football as an event, an exciting spectacle. "What we set out to do was to get the audience involved emotionally," Arledge emphasized. "If they don't give a damn about the game, they still might enjoy the program." College football ratings soared under Arledge's artistry.

Arledge also proved the accuracy of his philosophy when he launched "ABC's Wide World of Sports" in 1961. Using the catchy slogan suggested by announcer Jim McKay, "the thrill of victory, the agony of defeat," Arledge broke most of the accepted rules of sports broadcasting, including giving network coverage to sports events of limited importance because they could be used to fill airtime at little cost. The program featured track meets from Des Moines, rodeos from Cheyenne, golf from Scotland, bowling tournaments from Little Rock, mountain climbing from the Alps, baseball from Japan, surfing from Maui. . . .

Arledge was also the first producer to recognize that an event need not be broadcast live to attract an audience; he and his associates discovered the delightful fact that a taped replay, properly edited, could actually increase the entertainment value of an event. Thus a 200-mile automobile race could be compressed into a few minutes, enough time to show a spectacular accident, the leaders jockeying for position, a grimy pit crew changing tires, and the inevitable waving of the checkered flag. Similarly a 26-mile marathon could be encapsulated into a few minutes with careful editing: brief glimpses of the start of the race, a few sympathetic shots of agonizing runners hitting the dreaded "wall," and coverage of the near-exhausted leaders straining for the finish line.

Critics complained—with good reason—that Arledge stretched the definition of sport beyond the breaking point. By the time the program had reached its thirtieth anniversary in 1991, more than two hundred different so-called sports had been covered. Events never before considered for broadcasting appeared, if only briefly, on "Wide World": jai alai, triathalons, archery, dog sled racing, cat shows, bicycle racing, badminton, wrist wrestling, lumberjacks chopping down trees and balancing themselves on floating logs, horse shows, truck pulls, water skiing, chess, ice figure skating. You name it, and ABC probably proclaimed it to be a sport and put it on the tube. . . .

The Success of Monday Night Football

It was inevitable that such pioneering souls as Roone Arledge and Pete Rozelle would combine their talents. For several years Rozelle had tinkered with the idea of placing professional football on prime-time evening television, but he met resistance from tradition-bound television executives who could only conceive of professional football on Sunday afternoons. CBS, fearing women would not watch football, and more than satisfied with its high Monday night ratings, expressed no interest. NBC toyed with the idea for a time, only to back off for fear of angering late-night star Johnny Carson by having to air his show somewhat later than the traditional 11:30 EST start.

ABC's Arledge, however, viewed the concept as an opportunity to demonstrate his conviction that sport as entertainment could attract the casual fan, including women. For starters he decided to deploy numerous cameras around the stadium, instead of stationing three or four near midfield as had long been the norm for coverage of professional games. ABC staffers roved the sidelines with hand-held cameras in search of the unusual shot; cameramen mounted on motorized platforms followed the ball up and down the sidelines to provide graphic pictures of the violence on the line of scrimmage.

Special microphones picked up sideline noises (including a coach's occasional curse). Between plays, director Chet Forte frequently cut to a homemade sign draped around the stadium (which invariably mentioned ABC or one of its announcers), or to outrageously dressed fans (sacks over heads in New Orleans, a man wearing only a blue and orange barrel in sub-freezing Denver, dog masks in Cleveland). If none of these were available, Forte could always fall back on the time-tested shot of an attractive woman.

Football fans had never before witnessed such coverage. Instant replays from several angles became common, as did extensive use of "isolation" cameras. Dramatic visual effects resulted from an in-close picture of the football being smacked off the tee by a kicker's foot, a vivid shot of a player's bloody face, the gut-wrenching slow-motion pictures graphically showing the severe break of quarterback Joe Theisman's leg, or several replays of a referee's blown call. All of this and more was accompanied by Cosell's biting commentary or the irreverence (and frequent irrelevance) of Don Meredith's down-home observations. On occasion Meredith, fortified by a cocktail or two, would break into dubious song. . . .

"Monday Night Football" rewrote the rules about sports television and assured Roone Arledge a central place in the history of broadcasting. The program became an American institution, and although the fascination slowly wore off as the cast of characters in the broadcast booth changed, its ratings steadfastly remained high after both Cosell and Meredith had departed. . . .

While Roone Arledge revolutionized the way America spent its Monday nights, Pete Rozelle used television to create a new American national holiday—Super Bowl Sunday. The power of television inspired this uniquely American institution, although at the time of its creation in 1967 no one, not even the creative Pete Rozelle, could have anticipated the impact of the game. Born of the merger of the American and National Football leagues—for which Rozelle successfully lobbied Congress for another exemption to antitrust laws—it became within a few years the most single important sporting event in the United States, easily surpassing the World Series in popularity. By the early 1980s more than 50 percent of the

American people watched the game. Rozelle gave the game an initial aura of grandeur when he decided to number the games with Roman numerals (e.g., Super Bowl XXII), and he and the television executives of NBC and CBS (which alternatively broadcast the game until 1982) provided immense public relations hype during the two weeks leading to the game. . . .

The Super Bowl became the quintessential made-for-television event. Newspapers published suggested menus and recipes for Super Sunday parties. Estimates on the total amount of money bet on the game, legally in Nevada or illegally everywhere else, reached to several hundred million dollars. Rozelle's legendary pregame reception hosted six thousand very important people. It became a spectacle of spectacles. Many felt the pregame hype and media overkill overshadowed the game itself because most of the games proved to be boring, lopsided affairs, but few people cared. By the mid-1980s advertisers willingly paid upward of $400,000 to broadcast a thirty-second commercial, a staggering figure that nonetheless doubled by 1993. When Rozelle admitted ABC to the network rotation to televise Super Bowl XVI in 1982 it had to pay the NFL an "admission fee" of $18 million! . . .

In Quest of the Golden Goose

Sports coverage entered into its golden age in the 1960s. Promoters and leagues extracted enormous sums from competing networks. . . . The establishment of an all-sports cable station, the Entertainment and Sports Network (ESPN), in 1980 added another important dimension to the commercialization of sports. Within a few years ESPN had penetrated 60 percent of the nation's homes and with its flair for using satellites and other advanced communications technologies, took sports broadcasting in significant new directions. Its entertaining and informative evening Sports Center news summary attracted a large and dedicated audience, and although it had to fill the many hours with reruns of golf matches, body building competitions, demolition derbies, and a seemingly endless parade of mind-numbing automobile races, it became a major force in the mid-1980s by signing large contracts with organized baseball and the NCAA to cover regular season basketball and several rounds of the postseason tournament.

The escalating size of contracts was staggering. Pete Rozelle, capitalizing on continued increased ratings, negotiated a five-year contract in 1982 with the three major networks that produced $2 billion—or $14 million per team per year—for the NFL. . . . ESPN moved aggressively in 1988 to compete with the major networks when it signed a $75 million contract to broadcast major league baseball five nights a week throughout several seasons, having previously enjoyed success with its telecasts of a few selected Sunday evening NFL games. . . .

The Rules of the Game

Although various leagues and sports enterprises benefited from the television revenue bonanza, they also had to pay a stiff price in return. By paying out enormous sums, television producers were in a position to demand major changes in the sports they covered to make them more palatable to their viewing audience. More significant, the requirements of commercial television even forced the rewriting of the rules and policies of the sports it covered. The importance and value of the television audience—and in particular the advertisers paying enormous sums—far outweighed that of the fans who paid money to attend the event in person.

Examples of the changes produced by television are seemingly endless. For example, because of the popularity of the forward pass with television audiences, professional football changed its rules on blocking and defensive play to give the passing offenses new advantages. It even moved the hash marks toward the middle of the field to give the quarterback a wider area to attack. Names were placed on the backs of players to help announcers and viewers identify players. One-minute time-out periods were extended to two minutes and their frequency increased to accommodate the growing number of commercial breaks. Professional football introduced the nonsensical two-minute warning—an additional break for commercials with two minutes left to play in each half. The impact on other sports was similar. Tennis, which enjoyed a spate of interest in the mid-1970s, rewrote its rules to include the tie-breaker as a means of determining the winner of a tied set instead of the frequently lengthy former means of requiring the winner to take two consecutive games. Women's professional tennis received an enormous financial boost when the makers of Virginia Slims cigarettes decided to sponsor a series of tournaments as a means of getting its name before the viewing public after the Federal Communications Commission forbade cigarette advertising; in return the women's tour had to endure charges of hypocrisy for accepting enormous sums from a company whose product was deemed harmful to the health of its users. In response to the dictates of television, professional golf dropped its eighteen-hole playoff (held on Mondays) as a means of settling ties for the more dramatic one-hole playoff that could be televised live before the high-revenue Sunday evening programs commenced. The NBA, discovering that only playoff games could generate decent television audiences, thereupon expanded its postseason playoffs to include two-thirds of all the teams; what was once considered to be a "winter" sport now ended its interminable championship marathon in mid-June.

Even the game most steeped in tradition was not immune. In 1969 major league baseball opted for a playoff between the new "division" champions for similarly greedy reasons—increased television revenue. It also horrified baseball purists by moving the World Series from the traditional autumn afternoon to prime time to increase television ratings. . . .

Television also served to nationalize sport. Premier sportscasters like Joe Garagiola, Curt Gowdy, Dick Enberg, John Madden, and Jim McKay now commanded six- and even seven-figure salaries; some, like Howard Cosell, became news makers in their own right. New and often unusual loyalties sometimes resulted: a visitor in the 1980s to the small isolated mining town of Austin, Nevada, was bemused to learn that most of the town's residents were ardent Atlanta Braves fans. They followed the Braves because their new satellite dishes picked up Ted Turner's Atlanta "super station," which broadcast the Braves' games. Similarly, the sale of Chicago station WGN programming to cable companies created a national fan base for the Chicago Cubs. The Dallas Cowboys became known as "America's team," a result of their sustained high profile on national television. College basketball coaches in western states loudly cried foul in the 1980s when the Big East Conference negotiated major television contracts that placed their teams on national telecasts with greater frequency. Much to their dismay, these coaches found they were losing many top West Coast recruits to Big East teams, the primary reason being the lure of increased national television exposure.

With the development of satellite technology, sports bars flourished, offering their patrons several large-screen television sets that showed several different sporting events simultaneously. Television commercials even took on lives of their own. Setting the standard in this regard was the often humorous use of former sports stars by the Miller Brewing Company to promote beer. Winning, always important to Americans, became even more important as fans everywhere dreamed of becoming "number one." College basketball coaches found lucrative incentive clauses in their contracts if their teams reached certain levels of the NCAA basketball tournament; football coaches were similarly rewarded if their team appeared in a postseason bowl game because television rights to these games helped increase the revenue for participation in a major bowl team to several million dollars—for one game. Coaches now felt extreme pressure to take their team to a postseason tournament or bowl game; athletic directors even included such hoped-for income into their annual budgets. "The college game is just like the pro game," one disgruntled veteran college basketball coach complained. "It all changed with all that big TV money. The need to win is tremendous. A monster has been created that people just can't keep feeding."

A Force for Change

Monster or munificent benefactor? Television has been both of these and much more. On one hand it has brought sports to the nation, producing an endless parade of enjoyment in the form of athletic competition at all levels. On the other hand it has converted both professional and amateur athletics into major business enterprises, exploiting higher education and individual athletes in a shameful fashion. It has also demanded and received major changes in the sports themselves. Not surprisingly, television has produced a new set of values and attitudes among spectators and participants alike. For better or worse, television has been a dominating force in American sports in the second half of the twentieth century.

The Growing Popularity of Extreme Sports

Joan Raymond

Joan Raymond is a writer for *American Demographics* magazine. In the following article, she examines how extreme sports such as skateboarding and snowboarding have captured the attention of fans, television producers, and corporate sponsors since the early 1990s. Ratings for the X Games, which debuted on ESPN in 1995, and the Gravity Games, which debuted on NBC in 1999, have steadily risen, according to Raymond. Extreme athlete-celebrities such as skateboarder Tony Hawk are increasingly recognized by mainstream audiences, and corporations are seeking to cash in on the marketing potential of extreme sports. Raymond writes that extreme sports are most popular with young males, who may associate such sports with individualism and social rebellion.

ANDREW ROYAL ISN'T YOUR TYPICAL COUCH potato. The 26-year-old from Cleveland, who works two jobs to finance his new mortgage payments, rarely sits glued to the tube—even when his hometown team, the Cleveland Browns, is playing on Monday Night Football. But when the X Games or the Gravity Games are on, Royal not only makes time to watch, he actually schedules his day around what's on TV. "These athletes are so on the edge that it actually makes watching TV enjoyable," says Royal, who hung up his skis

■

Joan Raymond, "Going to Extremes," *American Demographics*, vol. 24, June 2002, pp. 28–30. Copyright © 2002 by Primedia Business Magazines & Media, Inc. Reproduced by permission.

more than 10 years ago in favor of a snowboard. "Extreme sports are my Monday Night Football."

More than a Passing Fad

For those who still think a half pipe is something you light up, wake up and smell the Mountain Dew. Extreme sports, once considered the sole province of the multi-pierced, tattooed slacker, have entered the mainstream. These high-intensity, individualistic sports, which involve everything from the ultra-hip snowboarding to Moto-X (a strange, scary contest that has motorcyclists attempt ski jumps) have encroached upon traditional sports—especially group sports—in popularity. While Monday Night Football, for example, has recently struggled for an audience, viewership has steadily increased each year for such sports events as the X Games on ESPN and the Gravity Games on NBC. "These new sports are an authentic slice of the wider youth culture and not just a fad," says Harvey Lauer, president of American Sports Data, Inc. (ASD), a sports marketing research company in Hartsdale, N.Y.

This youth culture consists of some 58 million Americans between the ages of 10 and 24. Horizon Media Research in New York City estimates this group's annual buying power at more than $250 billion. That's one reason why giants such as PepsiCo, AT&T Broadband, Motorola, Ford and Morningstar Foods—and even the U.S. Marines—have focused a chunk of their marketing budgets on capturing the elusive Gen X and Gen Y male consumers, who make up the bulk of extreme sports aficionados. PepsiCo's Mountain Dew, for example, has been a sponsor of the X Games, widely considered the Olympics of the extreme sports world, and the Gravity Games. . . .

Introduced in the 1960s, Mountain Dew was perceived as a hillbilly drink, says Dave DeCecco, spokesman for PepsiCo. That changed in 1992, when "Do the Dew" was born. The edgy ads, showing people engaged in various extreme activities, made Mountain Dew the fastest-growing soft drink of the 1990s. "The involvement was a natural extension of our advertising," DeCecco says. PepsiCo reports that the number of teens who said "Mountain Dew is a brand for someone like me" increased 10 percentage points between 1998 and 2001.

In an otherwise anemic sports-viewing market, extreme

sports have a hardy following. Although they can't match the numbers of Monday Night Football, ratings for the X Games and Gravity Games are rising—albeit from a much smaller base. Monday Night Football is one of the strongest sports broadcasting franchises, often ranking among the top 10 prime-time programs. But the show's standing has been declining for several years: Ratings for the ABC staple fell to an average of 12.7 percent of the nation's 100-million plus homes with televisions in 2000, and then fell to 11.5 percent in 2001, according to Nielsen Media Research. By contrast, the 2001 Gravity Games, held in Providence, R.I., averaged a 1.7 household rating—which corresponds to about 2 million households—up from 1.6 in 2000. The Winter X Games VI held in Aspen, Colo., in 2002, resulted in record viewership for ESPN and ESPN2: The telecast on February 3, 2 P.M. Eastern time, on ESPN, scored a 1.04 rating (894,640 households), making it the highest-rated and most-watched Winter X Games telecast ever on the network. (The sports network has been televising the X Games for seven years.) In 2001, the Summer X Games VII, in Philadelphia, also posted increases. In an X Games record, the 2001 event attracted an average audience of 465,905, an increase of 48 percent over the prior year.

Moreover, the demos are young and male—an elusive target group for most marketers. The 2001 Gravity Games, for instance, attracted more male viewers, 18 to 34, than any other action sports program. Among males ages 12 to 17, the Gravity Games drew a 1.7 household rating, corresponding to more than 200,000 male teens, up from 1.2 in 2000. Among males ages 12 to 24, the games drew a 1.3 rating, nearly 320,000 males, up from 1.1 in 2000. 2001's Summer X Games had some big air too: Within the 12- to 17-year-old demographic, ratings were up 86 percent (to 0.93 from 0.50), about 219,000 boys and girls, while numbers for males ages 12 to 17 were up 72 percent (to 1.48 from 0.86), about 178,000 boys. Within the coveted 18- to 34-year-old male demographic, ratings were up 40 percent, nearly 330,000 young men (to 1.05 from 0.75). Compare those demos with baseball's median age of 46.4 or even ESPN's total-day median age of 40.7.

"This is a demographic sweet spot," says Brad Adgate, senior vice president and corporate research director at Horizon

Media. "The games are an incredible success story in combining sports with entertainment, while targeting a specific market. If you look at the continually increasing participation numbers in these sports, viewership is going to continue to grow. I'm an entrenched Baby Boomer, and even I know who Tony Hawk is."

For those who don't, Tony Hawk is the undisputed god of skateboarding, the most famous alternative athlete of all time. He's the guy who took the skateboard out of the closet, placing it into the hands of an estimated 8 million boys and girls, ages 7 to 17. Indeed, skateboarding, snowboarding and wakeboarding are among the fastest-growing alternative sports in the U.S., according to the 14th annual Super-study of Sports Participation, conducted by ASD, which surveyed 14,772 Americans nationwide.

Snowboarding—once the stepchild of the ski slopes—now claims 7.2 million participants, up 51 percent from 1999. The kindred activities of skateboarding and wakeboarding surged 49 percent and 32 percent, respectively (to 11.6 million and 3.5 million participants). The subgenre of "board" sports thus gets a clean sweep of the top three growth positions among all alternative sports. This has occurred as membership in team sports is declining. Participation in baseball is down 28 percent since 1987, to 10.9 million players. Basketball declined by 5 percent in 2000 and 17 percent from its 1997 peak. Since 1987, involvement in softball and volleyball has plunged by 37 percent and 36 percent, respectively.

Alternative Sports, Alternative Values

ASD's Lauer says that part of the growth spurt in extreme sports stems from a rejection of the traditional values reflected in team sports, like working together, character-building and group competition. Alternative sports, he points out, are "rooted in a diametrically opposite set of values," including fierce individualism, alienation and defiance. But as Maria Elles, ESPN X Games marketing manager says: "You don't have to have a tattoo to like an action sport. The athletes are really setting the trends."

Wherever bleeding-edge athletes go, marketers are sure to follow. As a first-time X Games sponsor in 2001, Hershey's was looking for a spot to sample its new single-serve Hershey's Milk. According to Patty Herbeck, marketing director for Dallas-based Morningstar Foods, which markets the Hershey's product, the X Games sponsorship fit into the company's overall sports marketing initiative targeting 16- to 19-year-olds. Hershey's ran spots on ESPN during the X Games—the first national advertising campaign for the product. It then followed up with print ads in *ESPN The Magazine* and an on-site sampling campaign that "was bang for the buck," says Herbeck, citing that demand for samples was so high that Hershey's couldn't keep enough milk on site during the games.

With all the emphasis on all things extreme, isn't there a chance that the buck-convention status the sports enjoy will soon be as appealing to the young male demographic as cricket? In any sport, there are the mainstream and then the core enthusiasts, who set the standard and push the envelope. If extreme sports start to lose the "how did they do that?" factor, the hard-core fan will simply "set another standard, which will then trickle down to the mainstream," says Bill Carter, the 33-year-old president of Fuse Integrated Marketing, a Burlington, Vt.-based company which designs sponsorship programs for marketers.

But Carter is confident that it will be a while before the mainstream demands more than big backside air, with frontside air, along with a McTwist and an Indy grab. "A lot of viewers of snowboarding don't have a clue about the names of the tricks," says Carter. "What they see on television are elite athletes who are doing something that nobody's ever done before. And when it comes to these kinds of athletes, that's not going to change."

2

EXAMINING POP CULTURE

Sports Reflect American Values

Baseball and the American Dream

Robert Elias

Robert Elias is a professor of politics at the University of San Francisco. In the following selection, he examines the various ways in which pro baseball represents the American Dream. For example, baseball is said to give all players an equal shot at success, to reward practice and perseverance, to foster a sense of community among players and spectators, and to promote honesty and fair play. Moreover, in its long history baseball has in some ways come to symbolize America as a nation.

However, Elias also points out some of the negative ways in which baseball reflects American values. For example, the egalitarian image that pro baseball established during the civil rights era is undermined by the exclusion of women from the professional ranks. Major League Baseball is also characterized by enormous economic inequities, among players, management, and different teams within the league. However, Elias expresses hope that baseball can overcome these problems and serve as a model for what American society can become.

HISTORIAN PETER BJARKMAN HAS WRITTEN THAT baseball "is a game which surely does not mean half of the things we take it to mean. [But] [t]hen again, it probably means so much more." So true. And for that reason, we can proclaim, unflinchingly, that baseball reflects some of the nation's no-

■

Robert Elias, "A Fit for a Fractured Society: Baseball and the American Promise," *Baseball and the American Dream: Race, Class, Gender, and the National Pastime*, edited by Robert Elias. Armonk, NY: M.E. Sharpe, 2001. Copyright © 2001 by M.E. Sharpe, Inc. Reproduced by permission.

blest aspirations. There's perhaps no better way to see them than to examine baseball's relationship to our quintessential national quest: the pursuit of the American dream. . . .

The American dream views the United States as the land of opportunity where sufficient dedication and hard work guarantees individual mobility and success, for natives and newcomers alike. Our land is a "melting pot" where people of all races readily commingle, and live and work together as a united citizenry. The dream promises wealth and riches for all who energetically seek them, regardless of one's class, gender, religion, and ethnicity. The path to success relies on vigorous competition in the free-market system where political freedoms protect individual choice, initiative, and participation, and ensure fairness, justice, and equality.

The Horatio Alger work ethic relies not merely on sweat but also on ingenuity. Those who effectively apply themselves can make their fortunes; everyone else will at least be middle class. The individual pursuit of material gains will enrich not only individuals but also the broader society. And beyond individualism, the dream offers God, family, and the nation. The American dream makes the country special: it nourishes the American people, it seduces foreigners to our shores, and it spreads the American way far beyond our own borders. . . .

A Field of Dreams?

With what ingredients of the American dream has baseball been associated? How has the game reflected the best in American culture? To begin with, baseball has been credited with promoting democracy and good government, and has been connected to political institutions from the White House to the Supreme Court. [Historian] Francis Trevelyan Miller claimed, "Baseball is democracy in action: in it all men are 'free and equal,' regardless of race, nationality or creed. Every man is given the rightful opportunity to rise to the top on his own merits. . . . It is the fullest expression of freedom of speech, freedom of press, and freedom of assembly in our national life." Baseball has been linked to the development of both community and individualism. While baseball helped us, after the Civil War, to solidify ourselves into a nation, "an accompanying industrial upheaval," according to David Voigt [author of *America Through Baseball*],

> destroyed the people's sense of community as a fixed place, and moved Americans to embrace collective symbols like the Flag, the Constitution, the Declaration of Independence, along with popular heroes to substitute a feeling of national community identity. . . . Having abandoned royal and aristocratic heroes, Americans took to glorifying the self-made man of the Industrial Revolution. The new pattern deified the myth of the ordinary man rising to the top, an image that reflected a deeply felt hope that the American people really do rule.

Baseball has been viewed as a fertile ground for that "self-made man." The game helps develop skills for individual success, especially the work ethic and other values for the business world. Business leaders have praised baseball as a model of competition. In the early twentieth century, *American Magazine* editorialized, "Baseball has given our public a fine lesson in commercial morals. . . . Some day all business will be organized and conducted by baseball standards." More recently, [in a 1987 *In These Times* article] baseball has been called one of "the last outposts in our high capitalist society of individual meritocracy," and when ballplayers cash in on their talents, [according to a 1977 *USA Today Baseball Weekly* article] it's considered a part of "the American way."

In his study of baseball in the Progressive era, Stephen Riess claims, "The national pastime was portrayed in such a way that it supplied some of the symbols, myths and legends society needed to bind its members together." Richard Crepeau has written that baseball "most typified American institutions and teachings in the 1920s and 1930s," including the values of democracy, opportunity, and fair play. As David Voigt has suggested, "Players found baseball to be a promising road to individual recognition. Perhaps as much as any institution, American baseball kept alive Horatio Alger's myth that a hungry, rural-raised, poor boy could win middle-class respectability through persistence, courage and hard work." And for those on the sidelines, baseball nevertheless served an important role in developing individual identities. The fan's affiliation with his or her team has often exceeded in vigor his or her attachment to church, trade, political party—all but family and country, and even those have sometimes emerged all wrapped up in baseball.

Baseball, according to Voigt, has also been considered "a primary vehicle of assimilation for immigrants into American society, and as a stepping stone for groups such as Irish-Americans, German-Americans, and Italian-Americans—each of which entered the professional ranks of the sport in waves between the 1870s and the 1930s. . . . The brilliant success stories of [various] . . . hyphenated Americans kept the myth of the American melting pot alive in baseball."

Likewise, leaders of immigrant groups advised their peoples to learn the national game if they wanted to become Americans, and foreign language newspapers devoted space to educating their readers about the American game. [Baseball historian] Harold Seymour has observed, "The argot of baseball supplied a common means of communication and strengthened the bond which the game helped to establish among those sorely in need of it—the mass of urban dwellers and immigrants living in the anonymity and impersonal vortex of large industrial cities. . . . With the loss of the traditional ties known in rural society, baseball gave to many the feeling of belonging." . . .

Baseball has been used to demonstrate the racial and ethnic mobility that occurs in an egalitarian, opportunity society, both for immigrants and natives alike. [*New York Times* writer] Buster Olney has observed:

> More than a half-century after Jackie Robinson broke baseball's color barrier, America celebrates his legacy, which is reflected in today's game. [Sammy] Sosa and pitcher Pedro Martinez are from the Dominican Republic, shortstop Omar Vizquel from Venezuela. Colorado's Larry Walker is Canadian. [Derek] Jeter's father is African-American and his mother is Irish. The Dodgers' Chan Ho Park is from Korea, Hideo Nomo is Japanese. [Mark] McGwire and . . . Tony Gwynn are both Californians. The lines, once hard and impenetrable, are all blurred. . . . When Orlando Hernandez, the defector from Cuba, signed with the Yankees, catcher Joe Girardi noted the variety of the New York pitching staff: Kansas City Irishman David Cone, Andy Pettitte

of French descent, the Panamanian-born Ramiro Mendoza, Hideki Irabu of Japan. And David Wells, Girardi mused, he's from Jupiter.

In addition, baseball has been viewed as scientific and well-constructed—a reflection of American ingenuity and a symbol of American progress and modernity. As Michael Novak has put it [in *The Joy of Sports*], "Baseball . . . is a cerebral game, designed as geometrically as the city of Washington itself, born out of the Enlightenment and the philosophies so beloved of Jefferson, Madison and Hamilton. It is to games what the *Federalist Papers* are to books: orderly, reasoned, judiciously balanced, incorporating a larger plan of rationality."

Baseball has been used to demonstrate the benefits of play, team spirit, and sportsmanship. Playing the game has been regarded as a preventative against things such as crime, violence, delinquency, and even the stresses of modern life. Baseball, it is said, promotes positive values such as honesty, fair play, wholesomeness, and other aspects of the American way. It has been associated with healthfulness, and especially with manliness. Baseball has been widely represented in our language and literature. It exudes beauty and grace, and carries an aesthetic appeal for many observers, who have described baseball as "poetry in motion," "a work of art," and "a form of music." The game has been linked to patriotism and nationalism, and has been thought to promote American prestige both at home and abroad. Baseball has often been associated with the armed services, and with enhancing America's mission around the world. For these and other reasons, baseball has been what Harold Seymour has called a "badge of Americanism." . . .

Second Thoughts on the Baseball Dream

Of course, baseball's long association with the American dream might also have a downside. It might mask some uncomfortable realities about both the national pastime and the American promise. . . .

Questions have been raised, for example, about continuing race problems in baseball. According to David Voigt:

> In both baseball and the broader society, ideals and realities have routinely clashed along economic class lines, but the gap

has been even more evident along racial and ethnic lines. The opportunities for some groups have been few rather than many, and for some races, virtually all access has been choked off for long periods . . . certainly, for African-Americans and Native Americans, and often . . . for Asian-Americans and Latino-Americans. . . . As some of the barriers to . . . the American dream have fallen in more contemporary times, we nevertheless often find, both inside and outside baseball, that progress . . . still [falls] well short of our American ideals.

. . . Some also worry about the lingering obstacles to women's participation in baseball. The writer Susan Berkson has written, "Ken Burns [in his *Baseball* book and documentary] calls baseball a metaphor for democracy. But he's wrong. Instead, it is a metaphor for sexism. The great theme is that it's a boys game; women have been shut out again and again." Although women have been much more involved in the sport throughout our history than we commonly understand, this discrimination against women remains largely true. . . .

In addition, economic inequalities often prevail in baseball on several different levels, between minor leaguers and major leaguers, between players and owners, between big market owners and small market owners, and so forth. As [sportswriter] John Thorn has suggested:

> The lie of baseball is that it's a level playing field. That there's equality. That all the inequalities in American life check their hat at the door. That they don't go into the stadium. That once you're there, there's a sort of bleacher democracy, that the banker can sit in the bleachers and converse with the working man next to him. This is a falsehood. You have class and race issues that mirror the struggle of American life, playing themselves out on the ballfields.

. . . According to Tom Goldstein [publisher of the baseball magazine *Elysian Fields Quarterly*], baseball is being run "by network executives, marketing consultants, and PR 'wizards.'" Thus, the "long-term *quality* of the game no longer matters; it's merely the short-term *perception* of how baseball is doing that's important." Goldstein argues, "Baseball is America's newly found 'cheap' natural resource. Our communities have become strip mines, and the fans are the precious commodity to be plundered."

The labor-management conflict in baseball in the early 1990s also took a significant toll. As [baseball writer] Leonard Koppett has suggested, baseball's

> inviolable connection to the past would be broken, and the separation of baseball business from business on the field would no longer be possible in [anyone's] consciousness. . . . [E]specially [for] those not involved in the business . . . the cancellation of the 1994 World Series was a breaking point. Popularity and prosperity returned quickly once play was resumed, but the nature of the baseball experience was altered forever. . . . Personalities and games became inextricably linked with dollars, [which] became a factor in understanding outcomes and one's reaction to the . . . games played.

Likewise, [editor of *Elysian Fields Quarterly*] Stephen Lehman has lamented the alarming and growing economic disparities in major league baseball. He resents the perpetuation, if not promotion, of those gaps by appeals to the American dream. Such appeals can be found, for example, in former Los Angeles Dodgers' manager Davey Johnson's recent reaction to concerns that rich teams (like his) are cornering the best baseball talent with high-priced contracts. "Parity is not the American way," according to Johnson. "The American way is to dominate somebody else.". . .

Lehman believes we're losing the baseball dream; owners have extorted cities and taxpayers for new ballparks, thus diverting scarce public resources, and yet their ability to field competitive teams remains just as unlikely as before. As Lehman argues, "In at least half the major league cities in America and Canada, there will be no hope and . . . no faith . . . [but rather] only the certainty of being dominated by the wealthy and powerful. And that is not a model for healthy competition. It is not the American (or Canadian) Way.". . .

Restoring Baseball's American Dream

How can we unleash the potential in baseball for progress while also harnessing its more manipulative or less constructive forces? For example, if Jackie Robinson opened baseball to people of color, and if Curt Flood returned some control of the game to the players, how and who can return the game, now, to the fans? Cal Ripken, Sammy Sosa, and Mark Mc-Gwire might have begun the process. Nevertheless, in our spectator culture, where most of us watch our games and our society passively on the sidelines, how can fans and citizens be brought more into the center of the action? As [journalist] Andre Mayer has argued:

> We need to get Americans involved again, paying attention, understanding what's going on. They don't have to be on the field, but they should be in the park, not just watching on TV. I mean this literally, because baseball has more than metaphoric meaning to American life. It is the backbone of our national culture, of our common mental discipline. What René Descartes is to France, Abner Doubleday is to America. Baseball inculcates the habits of mind essential to our survival as a free people.

Arguably, the present and future of our national pastime and of America are intertwined. America seems poorer without baseball on center stage. Can baseball regain its influence and importance in U.S. society? . . .

It's not clear whether [a solution] will emerge from baseball's ruling establishment. But a new direction for baseball can nevertheless also come from baseball players and their union, and from baseball fans and their communities. Baseball could provide initiatives to help reform not only the national pastime but also American society. It could lead the way on worker's rights and in revitalizing the labor movement. It could promote genuine racial equality and improve race relations. It could push for serious enforcement of antitrust laws and provide new models of public or cooperative ownership for teams and other corporations. It could concern itself with its consumers—the fans—as humans and not merely as commodities. It could promote new breakthroughs in women's access to the game and to sports and American institutions. It could be a progressive influence in America to push back the greed and conservatism of the 1980s and 1990s. It might even be a force for curbing aggression and promoting conflict resolution in U.S. foreign policy—such as the "baseball for peace" tours to

Central America in the 1980s and the recent Cuba-Baltimore Orioles exhibition series.

At its best, perhaps baseball is better than American society. As Reggie Jackson once suggested: "The country is as American as baseball." Baseball has within it the capacity to help make the American dream one that's more worth attaining, and to make it one that's far more accessible to far more people than the conventional American dream. There are disturbing signs that America is a culture in decline. The increasing attempts to impose the American way abroad seem correlated with an increasing tendency for Americans to question their society at home. Can baseball provide us some salvation? Perhaps society ought to be looking up to the best in baseball. As journalist Bill Vaughan once wrote, "What it adds up to is that it is not baseball's responsibility to fit itself into our frantic society. It is, rather, society's responsibility to make itself worthy of baseball. That's why I can never understand why anybody leaves the game early to beat the traffic. The purpose of baseball is to keep you from caring if you beat the traffic."

How can the national pastime help fulfill the American promise? John Thorn has put it this way:

> Fundamentally, baseball is what America is not, but has longed or imagined itself to be. It is the missing piece of the puzzle, the part that makes us whole . . . a fit for a fractured society. While America is about breaking apart, baseball is about connecting. America, independent and separate, is a lonely nation in which culture, class, ideology and creed fail to unite us; but baseball is the tie that binds. . . . Yet more than anything else, baseball is about hope and renewal . . . gloriously pulsing with the mystery of the seasons and of life itself. This great game opens a portal onto our past, both real and imagined . . . it . . . holds up a mirror, showing us as we are. And sometimes baseball even serves as a beacon, revealing a path through the wilderness.

For those of us pursuing a new and better American dream, it's a path we should all be gladly taking.

The Cultural Significance of Basketball

Todd Boyd and Kenneth L. Shropshire

Basketball is a mirror for American culture, assert Todd Boyd and Kenneth L. Shropshire in the following selection. For example, while the rivalry of Magic Johnson and Larry Bird in the 1980s reflected America's continuing racial tensions, Michael Jordan's fame and prominence in the media in the 1990s seemed to transcend race. The rise of the Women's National Basketball Association in the 1990s and the negative images surrounding many NBA players may indicate that gender and class issues have become more pressing issues for Americans. Whatever pro basketball symbolizes, the United States' decision in 1992 to allow "Dream Teams" of NBA players to compete in the Olympics has assured that, at least on the world stage, basketball is the sport that represents America.

Todd Boyd is a professor of critical studies at the University of Southern California and the author of *Am I Black Enough for You? Popular Culture from the 'Hood and Beyond*. Kenneth L. Shropshire is a professor of legal studies at the Wharton School at the University of Pennsylvania and the author of *In Black and White: Race and Sports in America*.

BASKETBALL IS PERFECTLY SUITED TO DEFINE American culture because of the ease with which it is repre-

■

Todd Boyd and Kenneth L. Shropshire, *Basketball Jones: America Above the Rim*. New York: New York University Press, 2000. Copyright © 2000 by New York University. Reproduced by permission.

sented through the media. By comparison, football seems never to be viewed in this manner. Although football has tremendous television viewership and huge revenues from ticket sales, the game is simply not as intimate as basketball. Unlike baseball and especially football, in basketball the players' faces are easy to see and thus easy to use in advertisements. Because of this intimacy, there is a clearer identification between fans and individual players, or at least with players as we perceive them to be.

The Most Media-Friendly Sport

The game is also fast paced and easily reducible to the television news format, highlighting dunks and three-point shots. Basketball blends with television like rock with MTV. In 1993 the television ratings for the NBA Finals were, for the first time, higher than baseball's World Series. Unlike baseball and football, basketball is a sport that came into its own in the television age. Baseball grew up in the golden age of radio, and many of those non-visual vestiges remain. Regarded as a sport of minimal national interest in the 1970s, basketball has become mainstream entertainment and popular culture in the 1990s and looks posed to broaden this appeal throughout the twenty-first century.

One can follow this transition by observing the game's escalation in media representation since the late 1970s. The 1979–80 finals between the Los Angeles Lakers and the Philadelphia 76ers were telecast at 11:30 P.M. on tape delay by CBS Sports. The event is now a multinight prime-time event. What was once "filler" on tape delay for CBS's notoriously abysmal late-night programming has become an integral part of prime-time network representation.

Baseball, in the interim, has steadfastly refused to change any rules to speed up the slow-moving game. Though an event such as the Sammy Sosa/Mark McGwire home-run race breathed new life into baseball—this, while basketball suffered labor strife and the retirement of its biggest star, Michael Jordan—basketball remains the media and pop-cultural darling of sports.

In the interest of demonstrating basketball's continued ability to transcend the world of sports, we focus on the late 1970s, when the league began its rise toward mass media popularity, through the present, when the political, social, and cultural changes in America have fundamentally altered the public presentation and reception of the game. This is also a time when America is undergoing a mass identity crisis of its own.

During the Reagan era, America entered a period of transition. The country's overall attempts at redefinition in the aftermath of significant historical events such as the Civil Rights and Black Power movements, feminism, Vietnam, Watergate, the continuing oil crisis, the decline of the cold war, and the necessity of learning to live in a high-tech, postindustrial economy created an environment where many of the commonly held tenets of our cultural identity were simply no longer viable. So much was in turmoil.

As these circumstances helped create an overall anxiety for a new identity, this desire for identity, in turn, opened up possibilities for new forms of culture to emerge to replace those that were suddenly becoming outdated. Over time, the media-friendly nature of basketball, like the sports of baseball and boxing before it, was able to fill a void and provide both a diversion and a realization of these societal circumstances. Basketball became prime time entertainment while simultaneously reflecting society in many ways.

For most of the twentieth century, baseball has been viewed as the sport that defines America. Baseball evokes tradition. Though this traditionalism still exists, especially in terms of baseball's internal politics, it is constantly being challenged, if not completely displaced, by the burgeoning prevalence of basketball.

Sports Heroes and the Politics of Race

While baseball remains the key vessel of sports nostalgia and tradition, it is basketball that currently saturates popular culture and permeates our national identity. In this regard, it is not difficult to argue that basketball's Dream Team [as the 1992 U.S. Olympic basketball team, the first to include professional players, was called] has become a most glaring sign of American identity in the highly nationalistic discourse that surrounds the Olympic Games. Nor is it unreasonable to assert that the cult of personality that often defines players as different as Michael Jordan and Dennis Rodman is equivalent to that of the most popular Hollywood celebrities.

This has been a shift from the largely white, working-class, conservative discourse of baseball, focused on icons such as Babe Ruth and Joe DiMaggio. These men were regarded as central to American culture and its representation of itself. The contemporary politics of basketball, as an enactment of popular culture and national identity, offers an opportunity to expose what appears to be a dissolution of the ideals of power and dominance in sports so long associated with white masculinity.

Sports has always been able to produce celebrities who assume larger-than-life proportions and occupy positions as icons of American culture. A closer look at the most significant of these icons over time reveals an interesting pattern. Whereas Babe Ruth's massive appeal as both a baseball player and a cultural symbol defined the early part of the twentieth century, and Muhammad Ali's politics of resistance defined the volatile 1960s and early 1970s, the present ubiquity of Michael Jordan, even in retirement, is perfectly suited for the media saturation of today.

Just as Ruth and baseball aligned perfectly with the white, working-class origins of a large segment of Americans, and Ali represented an evolving American position of racial politics and defiance of authority, Jordan embodies the postintegration moment when race, especially blackness, increasingly informs cultural dialogue, at the same time, paradoxically, rendering race largely invisible within the fabric of sports. Jordan's overall image, while popular, is one devoid of the character substance and specific cultural identity so integral to both Ruth and Ali. In this regard, Jordan's appeal has often been defined as raceless. His seemingly vapid, overmediated image is quite consistent with the void that tends to define much of contemporary American culture.

Consider Jackie Robinson's symbolic "breaking of the color line" in baseball, one of the central events in the public desegregation of American society. Though Robinson's acceptance into the major leagues in 1947 in no way eliminated racism, it certainly suggested to a postwar society that, as Sam Cooke sang, "a change is gonna come."

Serving as a precursor to the Civil Rights movement of the 1960s, Robinson's suggestive entry into one of this country's strongest, most conservative institutions demonstrated that race was inseparable from the progression of American cultural history. But in the same way that Robinson's break offered possibilities, Jordan's dominance and his suggested racelessness are an important prism with which to view contemporary society through basketball.

Bird vs. Johnson

From the mid-1960s, African American players were increasingly allowed into major college basketball programs. This is highlighted by the all-black Texas Western starting team that defeated all-white Kentucky in the 1966 National Collegiate Athletic Association (NCAA) championship game. Southern universities began recruiting blacks, and soon the college game was dominated by blacks.

In addition, the upstart American Basketball Association (ABA), which merged with the NBA in 1976, featured a large percentage of African American players and a style of play that closely resembled playground basketball, which is very much in line with the impulses of the black aesthetic. The ABA led in moving the game away from stiff two-handed set shots and bounce passes to behind-the-back alley-oop passes and 360-degree slam dunks. Blackness thus became normalized in discussions about basketball, and the sport was soon to be, in the words of Larry Bird, a "black man's game."

The postintegration era gained momentum at the end of the 1970s and beginning of the 1980s. Following on the heels of the 1960s push for integration and the 1970s attempt at "affirmative action," in the 1980s basketball became increasingly visible in popular culture, and reflective of the nation's racial conscience. The 1979 NCAA championship game featured the Michigan State Spartans and Magic Johnson against Indiana State and Larry Bird. This game signaled the beginning of a rivalry that would spill over into the pros and in some ways marked the dawning of a new era in basketball. As Johnson was drafted by the Los Angeles Lakers and Bird by the Boston Celtics, the tone was set for a narrative of race, history, and evolving social concerns that would play themselves out on the basketball court for much of the next decade.

Johnson's Lakers played in the entertainment metropolis of

Los Angeles. With the star of the team appropriately dubbed Magic; the coach, Pat Riley, representing the ultra-hip exterior of Hollywood celebrity; and their style of play referred to as "Showtime," Los Angeles contrasted starkly with the more traditional city of Boston and its working-class idea of substance-over-style basketball. Further, Boston's enthusiasm for a basketball team dominated by white players seemed to echo its racial politics. Boston and thoughts of busing and racial intolerance go in lockstep. Placing a predominantly white team on the parquet floor took a concerted effort, considering the high percentage of African Americans who play the sport.

This battle between Magic and Bird allowed for a displacement debate about race and masculinity present in sports since the days of boxer Jack Johnson and his legendary fights against several "great white hopes." To side with the Lakers or the Celtics was to embrace a racial position and a specific set

The Cultural Significance of Michael Jordan

Among the spectacles of media culture, Michael Jordan is a preeminent figure. As an NBA superstar, Jordan was the very picture of grace, coordination, virtuosity, and all-around skill—adeptly marketed to earn a record salary and endorsements. Jordan received $30 million to play for the Chicago Bulls in 1997 and $33 million in 1998; he earned more than $40 million in endorsements and promotions in 1995, making him the highest paid athlete in the world. Moreover, he reaped more than $45 million in endorsements in 1996, continuing his position as the world's highest paid athlete. In June 1998, *Fortune* magazine estimated that Jordan had generated more than $10 billion during his spectacular professional career in terms of an increase in tickets sold, television advertising revenue, increased profits of products Jordan endorsed, basketball merchandising exploiting Jordan's figure, and his own films, busi-

of cultural politics. As race is in some way endemic to every-thing in American society, the staging of these racial concerns through basketball allowed for a creative outlet with which to discuss cultural identity in not-so-obvious terms. The battles between Magic and Bird, L.A. and Boston, black and white, could be described as the late twentieth century's version of an acceptable race war.

Transcending Race

Yet the representation of the Midwest and the urban identity of postindustrial Detroit through the Detroit Pistons in the late 1980s offered a challenge to the East/West dichotomy. The self-proclaimed "Bad Boys," the Pistons, used a solid de-fense and what many would consider roughhouse tactics to es-tablish their place among the league's elite. Their style, often dismissed as overly aggressive, if not violent, was quite consis-

nesses, and product lines. Jordan *is* big business and has accelerated the trends toward the implosion of business, entertainment, and sports.

His Airness, a popular nickname for "the man that flies," thus epitomizes the postmodern sports spectacle both on the playing field and in advertisements and media spectacles. The Michael Jordan spectacle implodes athletic achievement with commercialization, merging his sports image with corporate products, and making Jordan one of the highest paid and most fecund generators of social meaning and capital in the history of media culture. He is the iconic exemplar of the media/sports spectacle, the ob-session with winning and success, and the quest for un-imaginable wealth that were defining cultural features of the last two decades of the twentieth century.

Douglas Kellner, "The Sports Spectacle, Michael Jordan, and Nike: Unholy Alliance?" *Michael Jordan, Inc.: Corporate Sport, Media Culture, and Late Modern America*, David L. Andrews, ed. Albany: State University of New York Press, 2001.

tent with the image of the city itself. Detroit, the original murder capital, has long been the epitome of urban blight in the minds of many Americans. The city's large African American population and identity facilitated an image that worked perfectly with the less glamorous style of the Pistons.

By the early 1990s, the Lakers, Celtics, and Pistons were losing their dominance to Michael Jordan and the Chicago Bulls. Jordan and his team ascended to prominence on the premise of transcending race. Jordan's ability to cross traditional boundaries owed a lot to the mass-media popularity of his non-threatening image, and the game's relegation of racial politics to the sidelines, so to speak, demonstrates a new series of concerns for the 1990s.

The shift from a covert discourse about race, which has been fully normalized at this time, to a discussion about class, gender, and even sexuality defines the present agenda in professional basketball. The popularity of the Women's National Basketball Association (WNBA) and women's basketball in general helps expand these possibilities well into the future. These issues are equally instructive in commenting on the American character. . . .

Further, a generation gap has developed in basketball that continues to exist today. This is articulated largely in class-specific terms. With arguments similar to those made against gangsta rap, the present generation of NBA stars are depicted as synonymous with greed, arrogance, selfish individualism, and an overall disrespect that has often embarrassed the "positive image"–driven league. Consider for a moment the fallout around Allen Iverson's reported comments to Michael Jordan that he doesn't respect anyone. This, for many, was tantamount to blasphemy.

Basketball and America on the World Stage

Another example of this generation gap appears when contrasting the first two installments of the Dream Team. The initial team centered on Magic, Jordan, and Bird, who were the beacons of nationalist glory. With the exception of Charles Barkley elbowing a much smaller Angolan player and later joking that the Angolan might have been carrying a spear, the Dream Team rode a crest of popularity that forever enshrined them in the annals of American history. The second incarnation of the team was to play in the 1994 world championships.

This team, which featured young players such as Shawn Kemp, Derrick Coleman (once a *Sports Illustrated* cover subject for a story that decried this new generation of player), and Larry Johnson, turned the games into a playground carnival, often hanging on the rim, grunting, taunting, and displaying an overall disregard for the unspoken rules of basketball social etiquette, particularly in the international realm—behavior for which they were criticized for years after the games were over. Their style of play was such that the older generation's problem child, Barkley, was transformed from a rebel to an elder and became a frequently outspoken critic of their youthful folly.

Basketball has become the preeminent American sport. An analysis of viewership, endorsement power of individual athletes, and the pervasiveness of the game globally all begin to point to basketball as more culturally significant than baseball and football, especially in contemporary society. Baseball has the history and football certainly still plays a prominent role in contemporary America, particularly in terms of the numbers of spectators, both in the stadiums and at home watching. Yet basketball assumes a larger place than either in the lexicon of popular culture throughout the world. . . . When you consider that a sport once dismissed as a "black man's sport" has come to represent America worldwide, then it is obvious that, if nothing else, the old order has been replaced.

Masculinity as Portrayed on Sports Television

Michael A. Messner, Michele Dunbar,
and Darnell Hunt

In the following essay, three researchers report on
their study of sports television programs such as
ESPN's *SportsCenter* and TNT's *Monday Night Nitro*
wrestling as well as football, basketball, and baseball
broadcasts. The researchers reached several conclu-
sions on how masculinity, violence, race, and gender
are presented in coverage of sports. They found, for
example, that women and minorities are underrepresented in sports television and that the media's coverage of sports encourages violence and other aggressive
behavior. The researchers conclude that mainstream
pro sports reinforce prevailing, and often harmful,
stereotypes about what it takes to "be a man."

Michael A. Messner is a professor of sociology
and gender studies at the University of Southern California. His books include *Power at Play: Sports and
the Problem of Masculinity* and *Sex, Violence, and Power
in Sports: Rethinking Masculinity*. Michele Dunbar is a
graduate student in sociology at the University of
Southern California, and Darnell Hunt is a professor
of sociology at the University of Southern California.

A RECENT NATIONAL SURVEY [BY THE AMATEUR
Athletic Foundation of Los Angeles] found 8- to 17-year-old

■

Michael A. Messner, Michele Dunbar, and Darnell Hunt, "The Televised Sports
Manhood Formula," *Journal of Sport & Social Issues*, vol. 24, November 2000, pp. 380–
97. Copyright © 2000 by Sage Publications, Ltd. Reproduced by permission.

children to be avid consumers of sports media, with television most often named as the preferred medium. Although girls watch sports in great numbers, boys are markedly more likely to report that they are regular consumers of televised sports. The most popular televised sports with boys, in order, are pro football, men's pro basketball, pro baseball, pro wrestling, men's college basketball, college football, and Extreme sports. Although counted separately in the Amateur Athletic Foundation (AAF) study, televised sports highlights shows also were revealed to be tremendously popular with boys.

What are boys seeing and hearing when they watch these programs? What kinds of values concerning gender, race, aggression, violence, and consumerism are boys exposed to when they watch their favorite televised sports programs, with their accompanying commercials? This article, based on a textual analysis, presents the argument that televised sports, and their accompanying commercials, consistently present boys with a narrow portrait of masculinity, which we call the Televised Sports Manhood Formula.

The Study

We analyzed a range of televised sports that were identified by the AAF study as those programs most often watched by boys. Most of the programs in our sample aired during a single week, May 23–29, 1999, with one exception. Because pro football is not in season in May, we acquired tapes of two randomly chosen National Football League (NFL) Monday Night Football games from the previous season to include in our sample. We analyzed televised coverage, including commercials and pregame, halftime, and postgame shows (when appropriate), for the following programs:

1. two broadcasts of SportsCenter on ESPN (2 hours of programming);
2. two broadcasts of Extreme sports, one on ESPN and one on Fox Sports West (approximately 90 minutes of programming);
3. two broadcasts of professional wrestling, including Monday Night Nitro on TNT and WWF Superstars on USA (approximately 2 hours of programming);
4. two broadcasts of National Basketball Association (NBA)

play-off games, one on TNT and the other on NBC (approximately 7 hours of programming);

5. two broadcasts of NFL Monday Night Football on ABC (approximately 7 hours of programming); and

6. one broadcast of Major League Baseball (MLB) on TBS (approximately 3 hours of programming).

We conducted a textual analysis of the sports programming and the commercials. In all, we examined about 23 hours of sports programming, nearly one quarter of which was time taken up by commercials. . . .

Dominant Themes in Televised Sports

Our analysis revealed that sports programming presents boys with narrow and stereotypical messages about race, gender, and violence. We identified 10 distinct themes that, together, make up the Televised Sports Manhood Formula.

White males are the voices of authority. Although one of the two SportsCenter segments in the sample did feature a White woman coanchor, the play-by-play and ongoing color commentary in NFL, wrestling, NBA, Extreme sports, and MLB broadcasts were conducted exclusively by White, male play-by-play commentators. . . .

Sports is a man's world. Images or discussion of women athletes is almost entirely absent in the sports programs that boys watch most. SportsCenter's mere 2.9% of news time devoted to women's sports is slightly lower than the 5% to 6% of women's sports coverage commonly found in other sports news studies. In addition, SportsCenter's rare discussion of a women's sport seemed to follow men's in newsworthiness (e.g., a report on a Professional Golfers' Association [PGA] tournament was followed by a more brief report on a Ladies Professional Golf Association [LPGA] tournament). The baseball, basketball, wrestling, and football programs we watched were men's contests so could not perhaps have been expected to cover or mention women athletes. However, Extreme sports are commonly viewed as "alternative" or "emerging" sports in which women are challenging masculine hegemony. Despite this, the Extreme sports shows we watched devoted only a single 50-second interview segment to a woman athlete. This segment constituted about 1% of the total Extreme sports programming and, significantly, did not show this woman athlete in action. . . .

Men are foregrounded in commercials. The idea that sports is a man's world is reinforced by the gender composition and imagery in commercials. Women almost never appear in commercials unless they are in the company of men. . . .

Women are sexy props or prizes for men's successful sport performances. Although women were mostly absent from sports commentary, when they did appear it was most often in stereotypical roles as sexy, masculinity-validating props, often cheering the men on. For instance, "X-sports" on Fox Sports West used a bikini-clad blonde woman as a hostess to welcome viewers back after each commercial break as the camera moved provocatively over her body. Although she mentioned the show's sponsors, she did not narrate the actual sporting event. The wrestling shows generously used scantily clad women (e.g., in pink miniskirts or tight Spandex and high heels) who overtly displayed the dominant cultural signs of heterosexy attractiveness to escort the male wrestlers to the ring, often with announcers discussing the women's provocative physical appearances. . . .

Whites are foregounded in commercials. The racial composition of the commercials is, if anything, more narrow and limited than the gender composition. Black, Latino, or Asian American people almost never appear in commercials unless the commercial also has White people in it. . . .

Violence and Aggression

Aggressive players get the prize; nice guys finish last. Viewers are continually immersed in images and commentary about the positive rewards that come to the most aggressive competitors and of the negative consequences of playing "soft" and lacking aggression.

Commentators consistently lauded athletes who most successfully employed physical and aggressive play and toughness. For instance, after having his toughness called into question, NBA player Brian Grant was awarded redemption by Sports-Center because he showed that he is "not afraid to take it to Karl Malone." SportsCenter also informed viewers that "the aggressor usually gets the calls [from the officials] and the Spurs were the ones getting them." In pro wrestling commentary, this is a constant theme. The World Wrestling Federation (WWF) announcers praised the "raw power" of wrestler "Shamrock" and approvingly dubbed "Hardcore Holly" as "the world's most dangerous man." NBA commentators suggested that it is okay to be a good guy off the court but one must be tough and aggressive on the court: Brian Grant and Jeff Hornacek are "true gentlemen of the NBA . . . as long as you don't have to play against them. You know they're great off the court; on the court, every single guy out there should be a killer."

When players were not doing well, they were often described as "hesitant" and lacking aggression, emotion, and desire (e.g., for a loose ball or rebound). For instance, commentators lamented that "the Jazz aren't going to the hoop, they're being pushed and shoved around," that Utah was responding to the Blazers' aggression "passively, in a reactive mode," and that "Utah's got to get Karl Malone toughened up." Sports-Center echoed this theme, opening one show with a depiction of Horace Grant elbowing Karl Malone and asking of Malone, "Is he feeble?" Similarly, NFL broadcasters waxed on about the virtues of aggression and domination. Big "hits"; ball carriers who got "buried," "stuffed," or "walloped" by the defense; and players who get "cleaned out" or "wiped out" by a blocker were often shown on replays, with announcers enthusiastically describing the plays. By contrast, they clearly declared that it is a very bad thing to be passive and to let yourself get pushed around and dominated at the line of scrimmage. Announcers also approvingly noted that going after an opposing player's injured body part is just smart strategy: In one NFL game, the Miami strategy to blitz the opposing quarterback was lauded as "brilliant"—"When you know your opposing quarterback is a bit nicked and something is wrong, Boomer, you got to come after him.". . .

This injunction for boys and men to be aggressive, not passive, is reinforced in commercials, where a common formula is to play on the insecurities of young males (e.g., that they are not strong enough, tough enough, smart enough, rich enough, attractive enough, decisive enough, etc.) and then attempt to convince them to avoid, overcome, or mask their fears, embarrassments, and apparent shortcomings by buying a particular product. These commercials often portray men as potential or actual geeks, nerds, or passive schmucks who can overcome their geekiness (or avoid being a geek like the guy in the commercial) by becoming decisive and purchasing a particular product.

Boys will be (violent) boys. Announcers often took a humorous "boys will be boys" attitude in discussing fights or near-fights during contests, and they also commonly used a recent fight, altercation, or disagreement between two players as a "teaser" to build audience excitement.

Fights, near-fights, threats of fights, or other violent actions were overemphasized in sports coverage and often verbally framed in sarcastic language that suggested that this kind of action, although reprehensible, is to be expected. For instance, as SportsCenter showed NBA centers Robinson and O'Neill exchanging forearm shoves, the commentators said, simply, "much love." Similarly, in an NFL game, a brief scuffle between players is met with a sarcastic comment by the broadcaster that the players are simply "making their acquaintance." This is, of course, a constant theme in pro wrestling (which we found impossible and less than meaningful to count because this theme permeates the show). We found it noteworthy that the supposedly spontaneous fights outside the wrestling ring (what we call unofficial fights) were given more coverage time and focus than the supposedly official fights inside the ring. We speculate that wrestling producers know that viewers already watch fights inside the ring with some skepticism as to their authenticity so they stage the unofficial fights outside the ring to bring a feeling of spontaneity and authenticity to the show and to build excitement and a sense of anticipation for the fight that will later occur inside the ring.

Pain and Sacrifice

Give up your body for the team. Athletes who are "playing with pain," "giving up their body for the team," or engaging in obviously highly dangerous plays or maneuvers were consistently framed as heroes; conversely, those who removed themselves from games due to injuries had questions raised about their character, their manhood.

This theme cut across all sports programming. For instance, SportsCenter asked, "Could the dominator be soft?" when a National Hockey League (NHL) star goalie decided to sit out a game due to a groin injury. Heroically taking risks while already hurt was a constant theme in Extreme sports commentary. For instance, one bike competitor was lauded for "overcoming his fear" and competing "with a busted up ankle" and another was applauded when he "popped his collarbone out in the street finals in Louisville but he's back on his bike here in Richmond, just 2 weeks later!" Athletes appear especially heroic when they go against doctors' wishes not to compete. For instance, an X Games interviewer adoringly told a competitor, "Doctors said don't ride but you went ahead and did it anyway and escaped serious injury." Similarly, NBA player Isaiah Rider was lauded for having "heart" for "playing with that knee injury." Injury discussions in NFL games often include speculation about whether the player will be able to return to this or future games. A focus on a star player in a pregame or halftime show, such as the feature on 49ers' Garrison Hearst, often contain commentary about heroic overcoming of serious injuries (in this case, a knee blowout, reconstructive surgery, and rehabilitation). As one game began, commentators noted that 37-year-old "Steve Young has remained a rock . . . not bad for a guy who a lotta people figured was, what, one big hit from ending his career." It's especially impressive when an injured player is able and willing to continue to play with aggressiveness and reckless abandon: "Kurt Scrafford at right guard—bad neck and all—is just out there wiping out guys." And announcers love the team leader who plays hurt:

> Drew Bledsoe gamely tried to play in loss to Rams yesterday; really admirable to try to play with that pin that was surgically implanted in his finger during the week; I don't know how a Q.B. could do that. You know, he broke his finger the time we had him on Monday night and he led his team to two come-from-behind victories, really gutted it out and I think he took that team on his shoulders and showed he could play and really elevated himself in my eyes, he really did.

Sports is war. Commentators consistently (an average of nearly five times during each hour of sports commentary) used martial metaphors and language of war and weaponry to describe sports action (e.g., battle, kill, ammunition, weapons, professional sniper, depth charges, taking aim, fighting, shot in his arsenal, reloading, detonate, squeezes the trigger, attack mode, firing blanks, blast, explosion, blitz, point of attack, a lance through the heart, etc.).

Some shows went beyond commentators' use of war terminology and actually framed the contests as wars. For instance, one of the wrestling shows offered a continual flow of images and commentary that reminded the viewers that "RAW is WAR!" Similarly, both NFL Monday Night Football broadcasts were introduced with explosive graphics and an opening song that included lyrics "Like a rocket burning through time and space, the NFL's best will rock this place . . . the battle lines are drawn." This sort of use of sport/war metaphors has been a common practice in televised sports commentary for many years, serving to fuse (and confuse) the distinctions between values of nationalism with team identity and athletic aggression with military destruction. In the shows examined for this study, war themes also were reinforced in many commercials, including commercials for movies, other sports programs, and in the occasional commercial for the U.S. military.

Show some guts! Commentators continually depicted and replayed exciting incidents of athletes engaging in reckless acts of speed, showing guts in the face of danger, big hits, and violent crashes.

This theme was evident across all of the sports programs but was especially predominant in Extreme sports that continually depicted crashing vehicles or bikers in an exciting manner. For instance, when one race ended with a crash, it was showed again in slow-motion replay, with commentators approvingly dubbing it "unbelievable" and "original." Extreme sports commentators commonly raised excitement levels by saying "he's on fire" or "he's going huge!" when a competitor was obviously taking greater risks. An athlete's ability to deal with the fear of a possible crash, in fact, is the mark of an "outstanding run": "Watch out, Richmond," an X games announcer shouted to the crowd, "He's gonna wreck this place!" A winning competitor laughingly said, "I do what I can to smash into [my opponents] as much as I can." Another competitor said, "If I crash, no big deal; I'm just gonna go for it." NFL commentators introduced the games with images of reckless collisions and during the game a "fearless" player was likely to be applauded: "There's no chance that Barry Sanders won't take when he's running the football." In another game, the announcer noted that receiver "Tony Simmons plays big. And for those of you not in the NFL, playing big means you're not afraid to go across the middle and catch the ball and make a play out of it after you catch the ball." Men showing guts in the face of speed and danger was also a major theme in 40 of the commercials that we analyzed.

The Televised Sports Manhood Formula

Tens of millions of U.S. boys watch televised sports programs, with their accompanying commercial advertisements. This study sheds light on what these boys are seeing when they watch their favorite sports programs. What values and ideas about gender, race, aggression, and violence are being promoted? Although there are certainly differences across different kinds of sports, as well as across different commercials, when we looked at all of the programming together, we identified 10 recurrent themes, which we have outlined above. Taken together, these themes codify a consistent and (mostly) coherent message about what it means to be a man. We call this message the Televised Sports Manhood Formula:

> What is a Real Man? A Real Man is strong, tough, aggressive, and above all, a winner in what is still a Man's World. To be a winner he has to do what needs to be done. He must be willing to compromise his own long-term health by showing guts in the face of danger, by fighting other men when necessary, and by "playing hurt" when he's injured. He must avoid being soft; he must be the aggressor, both on the "battle fields" of sports and in his consumption choices. Whether he is playing sports or making choices about which snack food or auto products to purchase, his aggressiveness will net him the ultimate prize: the adoring attention of conventionally beautiful women. He will know if and when he has arrived as a Real Man when the Voices of Authority— White Males—say he is a Real Man. But even when he has

finally managed to win the big one, has the good car, the right beer, and is surrounded by beautiful women, he will be reminded by these very same Voices of Authority just how fragile this Real Manhood really is: After all, he has to come out and prove himself all over again tomorrow. You're only as good as your last game (or your last purchase). . . .

This analysis gives us hints at an answer to the commonly asked question of why so many boys and men continue to take seemingly irrational risks, submit to pain and injury, and risk long-term debility or even death by playing hurt. A critical examination of the Televised Sports Manhood Formula tells us why: The costs of masculinity (especially pain and injury), according to this formula, appear to be well worth the price; the boys and men who are willing to pay the price always seem to get the glory, the championships, the best consumer products, and the beautiful women. Those who don't—or can't—pay the price are humiliated or ignored by women and left in the dust by other men. In short, the Televised Sports Manhood Formula is a pedagogy through which boys are taught that paying the price, be it one's bodily health or one's money, gives one access to the privileges that have been historically linked to hegemonic masculinity—money, power, glory, and women. And the barrage of images of femininity as model-like beauty displayed for and in the service of successful men suggests that heterosexuality is a major lynchpin of the Televised Sports Manhood Formula, and on a larger scale serves as one of the major linking factors in the conservative gender regime of the sports/media/commercial complex.

The Super Bowl and U.S. Chauvinism

Christopher R. Martin and Jimmie L. Reeves

The Super Bowl is the most popular annual sporting event in the United States. However, according to Christopher R. Martin and Jimmie L. Reeves, Americans are wrong to believe that the Super Bowl is popular on a global scale. The NFL states that almost a billion people watch the Super Bowl, yet has little evidence to support that estimate. International sporting events such as soccer's World Cup, the Cricket World Cup, and the Rugby World Cup can all boast far more viewers than the Super Bowl, and yet a minority of Americans follow these events. The authors maintain that the U.S. media's emphasis on the Super Bowl's supposed global significance reflects America's exaggerated sense of its importance in world affairs.

Christopher R. Martin is a professor of communication studies at the University of Northern Iowa, and Jimmie L. Reeves teaches courses on television and multimedia at Texas Tech University.

A LITTLE MORE THAN A DECADE AGO [IN 1989], AS the symbolic Berlin Wall was coming down, political leaders in the United States assured their citizens that a New World Order had come to fruition. This new, international, political arrangement would bring peace, of course, but more important was that it was implicitly an orderly peace—one which

■

would be administered and maintained by the United States, to the advantage of the United States. In other words, to the winner go the spoils.

Almost as quickly, the New World Order got disorderly. A Gulf War quelled, but did not dislodge Saddam Hussein's regime in Iraq; hundreds of thousands died in Rwanda as warring factions engaged in genocide; Pakistan and India rattled sabers with nuclear tests; and the worst act of terrorism visited U.S. soil, performed by a U.S. citizen. Daily NATO bombings of Serbia (including a few that were unfortunately aimed at the Chinese Embassy in Belgrade) failed to quickly halt ethnic cleansings in Kosovo, nor end the rule of the Serbian leader Slobodan Milosevic. And at a mostly white, upper-middle-class high school in Littleton, Colorado, two students turned guns and assorted weaponry on their peers and then themselves, ultimately killing 14 people and seriously injuring many more.

In countless ways U.S. political hegemony has been deflated in this New World Order. Although the U.S. side of the global economy mostly hums along, the problems of ungovernable international leaders, ineffective military interventions, and chronic internal violence make the U.S.'s favorite chant of 'We're Number One' ring a little hollow in the post–cold war era.

Into this tableau enters the Super Bowl. Each year, this supremely nationalistic event—the United States' most-watched television program—is marketed to people in the U.S. by the National Football League (NFL) and the mainstream national news media as an international affair. Worldwide audiences of nearly one billion are routinely announced in the pre-game hyperbole, and actively promoted during the broadcast. Many reports proclaim, as a public relations official for the NFL told us, that the Super Bowl 'is the greatest one-day sporting event around'.

But, is the Super Bowl the most super and most watched of sporting events in the world? What is the cultural significance of laying claim to being the sporting event with the most television viewers world-wide, especially in the historical conditions of this New World Order? . . .

With the overwhelming dominance of U.S. entertainment content—especially films, television, and music—around the globe, it is no surprise that the National Football League has worked to build a world-wide audience for American football and its premier television event. From the NFL's perspective, it is expanding the market for its product. Don Garber, then senior Vice President of NFL International, explained in 1999: 'We invest in a long-term plan to help the sport grow around the world. The vision is to be a leading global sport. We need to create awareness and encourage involvement.'

But the desire for global dominance of American football extends beyond just the NFL's profit-oriented interests. As an American cultural ritual, it is increasingly relevant (and increasingly common) that the Super Bowl is represented as the greatest and most watched sporting event on the planet. The enormous, *estimated* Super Bowl audience of between 800 million and a billion represents at least two competing ideals. On one hand, the Super Bowl's portrayal in mainstream U.S. news media as the leading international sporting event seems to combat post–cold war fragmentation by emphasizing increasing global unity, via a world-wide, shared Super Bowl experience. On the other, it is significant that this international unity is a unity not focused around World Cup soccer (which is *football* to the majority of the planet), but around *American football*, a U.S.-controlled export. Herein lies the great solipsism of the Super Bowl. To a large extent, Americans (and their mass media) cannot imagine—or do not wish to—the Super Bowl as being anything less than the biggest, 'baddest', and best sporting event in the world.

To imagine the Super Bowl as being this top sporting event is to ignore the counter-evidence of several other major sporting events:

- The estimated audience for the soccer World Cup (held every four years) is more than two billion viewers worldwide for the single-day championship match. In 1998 an estimated cumulative audience of 37 billion people watched some of the 64 games over the month-long event.
- The Cricket World Cup, held every four years (most recently in England in 1999) and involving mostly the countries of the former British Empire, has an estimated two billion viewers world-wide, but receives scant attention in the United States.

- Even the Rugby World Cup, also held every four years (most recently in Wales in 1999), claimed 2.5 billion viewers for its 1995 broadcast from South Africa.
- Canada, perhaps the country outside the U.S. most likely to adopt the Super Bowl as its own favorite sporting event—given Canada's geographic proximity, limited language barriers, and familiarity with the NFL, favors its own sports championship. The Grey Cup, the title game of the Canadian Football League, regularly draws three million viewers, more than the annual broadcasts of the Super Bowl and hockey's Stanley Cup final. Only the Academy Awards generate a larger Canadian television audience each year. . . .

On Sunday, 30 January 2000 the *Los Angeles Times* noted that 'the game will be broadcast on 225 television stations, 450 radio stations, and in 180 countries. The cliché about a billion people in China not caring is no longer applicable.' Yet the notion that the entire world pauses to pay homage to the Super Bowl is national mythology, continuously constructed via the NFL and the U.S. mass media. As we shall argue below, it is likely that more than a billion people in China do not even have the opportunity to care about the Super Bowl. . . .

Super Bowl Sunday Everywhere

That reports of the Super Bowl's international appeal are always estimated figures is disconcerting. While it is impossible to get an exact count of the viewers—the United States might have the most technically advanced television ratings systems, yet methodological deficiencies are commonly noted—the number of 800 million viewers is never documented in any way by the NFL nor the news media.

We were curious about this and approached the NFL's public relations department. According to one of the NFL's officials, the figure for the 800 million global audience for the Super Bowl is estimated, based on ratings-company figures from the U.S. (Nielsen) and from similar companies in each of the 180 other nations and territories that carried the game. Yet the estimates of the audience always are announced during the pregame hype, and are never—to the best of our knowledge and research—verified after the game (except for the U.S. numbers). Who could possibly check out these statistics, particularly if the NFL is not forthcoming? (Our NFL source seemed initially surprised that anyone would question the global audience figures, then just recited the same data.) The NFL official did acknowledge that the 800 million means that that number of people tuned in to watch at least a portion of the broadcast, not necessarily the entire one. This, of course, is similar to the American viewing experience; as ratings data indicate, many viewers tune out halfway through the game, particularly if the competition is lopsided.

Although the hyped international audience figures suggest that the whole planet is sharing the same American Super Bowl cultural experience, the time differential (particularly if 90 per cent of the international coverage is via a live feed, as the NFL claims) makes the viewing experience quite different. First of all, Super Bowl Sunday in the United States is Super Bowl Monday for the bulk of the world's population. With a kick-off time at approximately 6 P.M., Eastern Time in the U.S. (the time zone shifts, depending on the annual location of the game) on Sunday evening, game time for European viewers ranges from 12 midnight to 2 A.M., Monday morning. Kick-off is 7 A.M. Monday morning in Beijing, 8 A.M. in Seoul, and 9 A.M. in Brisbane. Thus the Sunday evening weekend party atmosphere that typifies the U.S. experience is awkwardly transplanted to an all-night ordeal in Europe or a Monday morning working day in east Asia and Australia. The Super Bowl's Sunday evening time slot—the evening with the heaviest television viewing in the U.S. each week—contributes to the Super Bowl's big viewership. But the Super Bowl's broadcast time in Europe, Asia, and Australia is clearly out of the realm of prime time and is one when few can afford to watch television.

Moreover, while the Super Bowl has free broadcast delivery in the United States, bringing the game to the more than 99 per cent of American households that have a television set, in other global markets the program's live distribution often comes only via paid cable or direct broadcast satellite television, both of which have a limited number of subscribers. The global audience is further limited by the fact that significant portions of the world's population are not even served by the cable or satellite signals that carry live feeds of the Super Bowl. . . .

The problem of access, however, does little to halt programming that suggests that the whole world stops for the Super Bowl. A 1½-min, prerecorded television package broadcast in the pre-game program for Super Bowl XXIX in 1995 is the most stunning example to date of U.S. solipsism with regard to the Super Bowl broadcast. The segment begins with an introduction by the ABC television network announcer Brent Musburger [voiced over live video of the shot from an airship of Miami's Joe Robbie Stadium at dusk, which later cuts to a shot of the field, with a pre-game show of balloons, music, and line-kicking women]:

> So there we are. A game that has grown so much over the last 29 years. Remember back in Super Bowl I? There were empty seats in the Los Angeles Coliseum. Seats were priced at $25 a piece. Now we're getting ready in Joe Robbie and the cheapest ticket is $200. The world awaits Super Bowl XXIX. And 174 countries will take the feed. And we estimate the audience for this Super Bowl will be in excess of 750 million. We hope everyone enjoys Super Bowl XXIX!

[The program then cuts to the prerecorded package, which begins with a spinning, animated globe and upbeat, suspenseful music. Then Musburger's voice-over resumes over an international montage of seven locations]:

> In Maine, they come in from the shore to watch the Super Bowl. [*Video:* screen text that says 'Cape Elizabeth, Maine' over a shot of a lighthouse on a rocky beach] The DMZ in Korea. Our young soldiers are ready. [*Video:* screen text that says 'The DMZ, Korea' over a shot of an American military check point in South Korea at the demilitarized zone border with North Korea] In San Diego, the Charger fans are euphoric. [*Video:* screen text that says 'San Diego, California' over a shot of whooping partiers on a yacht] Down under, they're ready. [*Video:* screen text that says 'Queensland, Australia' over a shot of a rugged Crocodile Dundee lookalike walking toward the camera] Greybull, Wyoming, where the cowboys come in to watch the game. [*Video:* screen text that says 'Greybull, Wyoming' over several men dismounting from their horses and walking into a barn] And in Antarctica,

they're bellying up. [*Video:* screen text that says 'McMurdo Station, Antarctica' over shot where two people dressed in parkas are watching a television outside while a lone penguin in the background falls and slides on his belly] In San Francisco, can the 49ers win it for a fifth time? [*Video:* screen text that says 'San Francisco, California' over a black (we note this because all other subjects shown except for a U.S. serviceman are white) man who puts a 49ers baseball cap on a black boy who is in a hospital bed; the man then turns on the television set; implicitly, they are father and son.]

Musburger then says, 'The stage is set.' The package then builds with a fast montage of each place just visited, as the music modulates to ever-higher keys:

- a night-time shot of Joe Robbie stadium (to give the illusion that this is live)
- a shot of cowboys in a Wyoming barn, crowded around the television set, with the same shot of the stadium on the screen
- the father and son in the hospital, with the same shot of the stadium on the screen
- the Australian takes a seat in his living room, explaining to his wife that this is 'American Footy—the Super Bowl'
- U.S. soldiers in a cafeteria line in Korea
- the mostly male partiers on the San Diego yacht
- the two researchers watching outside in Antarctica, high-fiving each other, and inexplicably drinking what looks like canned beer
- a middle-aged man with a golden retriever dog at his side, in front of a television set, with a warm mug of drink and a roaring fireplace in the background; man, dog, television set; no woman.

Finally, the music shifts to a tympani-heavy crescendo. Close-up shots are edited to the beat, and suggest a world-wide climax in anticipation of this great event:

- a cowboy close-up
- a smiling boy in hospital in a 49ers cap
- a smiling, pretty, young woman in a Chargers cap (the only woman emphasized in this entire package)
- an interested Australian watching the television set
- a captivated Antarctica viewer

- a close-up of the golden retriever's head, being patted by his master.

The montage dissolves to a live aerial shot of the stadium, Musburger says 'Super Bowl XXIX is coming up', and screen text appears that reads, 'SUPER BOWL SUNDAY EVERY-WHERE'.

The U.S.-centric thrust of this presumably international Super Bowl promotion is clear. The piece is mired in the old rituals of the Super Bowl: an emphasis on men, on white men, on white men in English-speaking countries and/or U.S. outposts, on U.S. military readiness, on rugged, masculine places like a rocky Maine coast, Wyoming ranches, the Australian outback, the icepack of Antarctica, and the dangerous DMZ. Women appear as the silent wife (Mrs Aussie) and as a cute, young thing (woman in Chargers cap). It is not surprising that a man's loyal hunting dog gets more screen time than a woman.

An Overestimation of Global Might

In a New World Order and an era of globalization that the U.S. seeks to master, imagining the Super Bowl as the premiere international television sporting event is a way to control 'our' American (U.S.) sport and 'our' superiority. But, in the solipsistic vision of the 1995 ABC television pre-game package, the imagined global audience looks largely like the imagined U.S. audience: people who either are Americans located at various points of the world, or people who look like white, middle-class Americans (the Australian couple), experiencing the telecast from the sofa in the living room, in the appropriate American style. This global vision contradicts the carnivalesque richness of the actual U.S. broadcast of the Super Bowl and the diversity (racial, ethnic, sexual, etc.) in the U.S. and the global population.

The sports historian Allen Guttmann has noted that 'a nation that exercises political and/or economic power usually exercises cultural power as well'. In a way, the symbolic nature of the Super Bowl works in reverse: the Super Bowl's high international stature is constantly reaffirmed in American culture as a self-comforting indication of the United States' political and economic power. Yet the vision of the Super Bowl's global status—particularly with its heavy reliance on symbols of masculinity, whiteness, and U.S. military might—is more Old World Order than New.

The fact that the Super Bowl is not the number one television sporting event may speak volumes about America's overestimation of its global might. It is not surprising, then, that soccer (the world's genuine top televised sporting event) remains a sport to ridicule for many people in the U.S. The *Los Angeles Times* in 2000 wryly stated that:

> the NFL estimates that more than 800 million people will watch the Super Bowl. An estimated 1.3 billion people watched the 1998 World Cup soccer final between Brazil and France. Can you remember the final score? Hint: one of the teams probably had 0.

The comment, a typical joke about soccer's low scoring, which presumably makes it boring for the sporting fan, allows American football fans to dismiss soccer as a sport that does not matter. Meanwhile, soccer continues to diffuse into U.S. culture much more quickly than the American football game extends globally.

Ironically, the hope for extending interest in professional American football in global markets requires the sport itself to be flexible—more malleable than the franchise managed closely by the NFL bureaucracy. But the game is likely to become less American and more internationalized if it should succeed in diffusing widely into other cultures, which is the case with the three leading world team sports—soccer, basketball, and volleyball. Thus the traditional mythic elements of NFL football that are so distinctly American are the same elements that prevent the Super Bowl from becoming the most-watched sporting event in the world.

3

EXAMINING POP CULTURE

Women and Minorities in Professional Sports

The Social Effects of Black Dominance in Pro Sports

John Hoberman

John Hoberman is the author of *Darwin's Athletes: How Sport Has Damaged Black America and Preserved the Myth of Race*. He argues below that the overrepresentation of black athletes in professional basketball and football perpetuates harmful racial stereotypes. While integrated professional sports undoubtedly have positive effects on race relations, Hoberman maintains that the belief that blacks are inherently better at sports encourages the misconception that there are biologically significant differences between blacks and whites. Worst of all, according to Hoberman, decades of "black dominance" in sports have left a generation of black children with only athletes as role models, and as a result many of them believe that academic achievement is only for whites.

THE SOMBER AND DETERMINED FACE OF A young black man stares out from a glossy magazine page while an equally resolute text lets us read his mind: "I can tolerate mistakes. But I cannot repeat them. I can grow." This, of course, is how point guards and wide receivers must think to survive in the tough games they play. Suddenly the attentive eye catches a glimpse of the dress shirt and tie that are just vis-

■

John Hoberman, "The Price of 'Black Dominance,'" *Society*, vol. 37, 2000, pp. 49–56. Copyright © 2000 by Transaction Publishers. Reproduced by permission.

ible at the bottom of the page, and cognitive dissonance sets in. For this positive thinker does not work for the National Football League (NFL) or the National Basketball Association (NBA). "I work for J.P. Morgan." This black man competes in banking, not basketball.

Clever advertising ploys like this illustrate one kind of progress in our society's unofficial and haphazard campaign to eliminate racial stereotyping from public spaces. For this well-dressed (and well-integrated) man represents the new entre-preneurial alternative to more familiar racial images—the sullen faces of black athletes we have seen looking tough and sweaty for the cameras that serve the marketing interests of athletic shoe companies and other sponsors. Any attentive ob-server of our advertising conventions will have noticed that basketballs and naked muscled torsos have long served as de facto signifiers of black masculinity for an audience that now includes almost anyone on earth. A few years ago, one black American long resident in Thailand sent me a letter in which he commented on the effects of this relentless barrage of black athletic images. Based on what their media showed them, he reported, South Asians had no reason to believe that African-American abilities extended beyond the world of sports.

While it is tempting to reply that Americans know better than that, given our knowledge of what black people have done in many fields of endeavor, our own domestic reality still resembles the global stage that presents NBA stars and other pop culture icons as representative African Americans. That is why relieving black men of the involuntary athletic identity that has been inflicted on them over the past one hundred years is part of the unfinished business that faces American so-ciety in the twenty-first century. . . .

The Price of "Black Dominance"

The essayist Gerald Early, for example, sees the black fighter as a symbol of "what it means to be a black American." "One could argue," he adds, "that the three most important black figures in twentieth-century American culture were prize-fighters: Jack Johnson, Joe Louis, and Muhammad Ali." This view finds support in a once-influential work of social science such as *The Mark of Oppression: Explorations in the Personality of the American Negro.* As the psychoanalysts Abram Kardiner and Lionel Ovesey listened to their black patients, they could observe the special role athletic heroes played in the minds of people whose lives had been deformed by a racial caste system. "Until recently," they wrote, "the Negro has had no real culture heroes with whom he could identify." They also concluded that athletes did not stimulate in black people the feelings of hostility and envy that could be directed at other black high achievers who had distinguished themselves in an academic setting. Whereas Joe Louis, Lena Horne, and Jackie Robinson could be "accepted by most Negroes as common ideal figures," the "educated Negro technician" occupied a tenuous position located somewhere between his fellow blacks and the dominant whites.

This oppositional relationship between black athletic and academic achievement has persisted during the age of "black dominance" in the sports world that began in the 1960s. One difference between the age of segregation and the post–Civil Rights era is that, during the later period, dreams of athletic stardom have induced many black children to reject educational opportunities that simply did not exist for those who grew up idolizing Jackie Robinson during the 1940s and 1950s. . . .

In *The Content of Our Character*, Shelby Steele's best-selling treatise on the emotional complexities of the African-American psyche, the author sees the focus on athletic achievement as a self-defeating defensive strategy, a way of staving off self-doubts that are continually being generated by academic failure. "Across the country thousands of young black males take every opportunity and make every effort to reach the elite ranks of the NBA or NFL," Steele writes. "But in the classroom, where racial vulnerability is a hidden terror, they and many of their classmates put forth the meagerest effort and show a virtual indifference to the genuine opportunity that is education.". . .

Unrealistic Faith in Sports

In 1997 Northeastern University's Center for the Study of Sport in Society reported that 66% of African-American boys between the ages of 13 and 18 believed that they were capable of supporting themselves as professional athletes. The prominent black psychiatrist and social activist Alvin Poussaint, a professor at Harvard Medical School, commented as follows: "There is an overemphasis on sports in the black community, and too many black students are putting all their eggs in one basket."

African-American doubts about the social utility of sport have never been as influential as the belief that black athletic achievement could advance racial justice and undermine racial prejudice. Often invoked but seldom examined, this faith in the black athlete as a politically invaluable role model and social resource became one of the ruling dogmas of American thinking about race and social progress and was eventually incarnated in the mythic person of Jackie Robinson. This faith in the social value of athletic achievement has been sustained by the persisting economic and educational disparities that separate African Americans from other ethnic groups in the United States. In a society where the net worth of the average black household is one-tenth that of its white counterpart, it is only natural that black parents and their children should vest disproportionate hopes in the sports entertainment industry's ability to provide for the athletic talent that sustains it. Nor are politically sophisticated people immune to the lure of this siren song. "We believe," Jesse Jackson wrote in 1993, "that sports can help change the despair in our communities into hope, replace low esteem with confidence and rebuild a true sense of community that transcends neighborhood and racial boundaries."

This declaration, for all its good intentions, revealed a striking lack of historical perspective. Here, at the end of the twentieth century, Jesse Jackson was invoking the millennial hopes for sport that the National Association for the Advancement of Colored People (NAACP) had proclaimed back in the 1920s and 1930s. Had the passage of most of a century not demonstrated what African Americans' engagement with sports could and could not do for them at different phases of their social development? Until the postwar period, racist restrictions on the education, professional training, and military service of African Americans had made athletes superlative examples of black achievement and qualities of character whites doubted they possessed.

Yet this emphasis on physical prowess also signified the underdevelopment of a people whose future prospects could not be built on the power of muscles. To be sure, what black athletic heroes such as Joe Louis and Jesse Owens did for African-American morale during the Jim Crow era should never be underestimated. But the social value of such performances during the subsequent era of integration has frequently been overestimated, and especially regarding the black stars of the 1990s. Young black athletes, Jesse Jackson said in 1995, "create a tremendous industrial base for black America. We cannot just settle for the pleasure of watching them perform." While the second of these assertions strikes me as correct, the first is inflated in the traditional fashion and overlooks the modern athlete's disconnect from social action of any kind apart from innocuous public service announcements. "You have athletes making absurd amounts of money, but why aren't they doing great things with it?" a reporter asked Charles Barkley of the NBA. The comment annoyed him, he said, because it was true. When Jayson Williams of the New York Nets announced a donation of $2.1 million to St. John's University at the end of 1999, this was apparently the second largest donation ever made to a university by any professional athlete.

Politically Inactive Black Athletes

Few statistics could convey as well as this one the sheer disinterest of black athletes in promoting social development, given that they earn an aggregate of around $1 billion a year. While that hardly constitutes an industrial base, Jesse Jackson is surely right to suggest that this group of black millionaires could do a lot more for their community. There are many black athletes, for example, who could have bailed out the NAACP when it faced bankruptcy a few years ago. The fact that not one of them responded to this nationally publicized financial emergency is one index of the decline of the black athlete as a significant actor on the stage of American race relations.

So which social or political roles are appropriate for the black athletic stars of the 1990s and beyond? Where are the barriers they might breach on behalf of racial progress? Who are the inheritors of Joe Louis and Jackie Robinson and Muhammad Ali? The absence of such sports figures is one result of the commercialization of the black athlete over the past generation. Whereas Jackie Robinson faced a society that did not want him, fifty years later Michael Jordan confronted an advertising market that could not get enough of him. His apolitical status came to be taken for granted as the entirely sen-

Race, Genetics, and Athletic Ability

Why are black athletes dominant in certain sports and underrepresented in others? Certainly one of the things that can be said with a degree of assurance is that there is no scientific evidence of genetic association or linkage between genes for individual and group athletic achievement among black Americans. We know as little about the contribution of genes to athletic ability as we do about the genetics of intelligence. Athletic ability is clearly a function of many genes in interaction with a number of other variables such as economic background, motivation, facilities, and coaching. How many genes may be involved in athletic ability is difficult, if not impossible, to determine since there is no way to separate out the contributions made by the aforementioned variables to sport performance.

Drawing links between genetic makeup and athletic ability is highly suspect, moreover, because, as . . . academicians have made plain through the years, it is highly questionable whether there is such a thing as a racial group considering the enormous lack of racial homogeneity within this country's black and white communities. The anthropometric differences found between racial groups are usually nothing more than central tendencies, and do not take into account wide variations within these groups or the overlap among members of different races. This fact not only negates any reliable physiological comparisons of athletes along racial lines, but makes the whole notion of racially distinctive physiological abilities a moot point.

David K. Wiggins, "Great Speed but Little Stamina: The Historic Debate over Black Athletic Superiority," *The New American Sport History*, S.W. Pope, ed. Urbana and Chicago: University of Illinois Press, 1997.

sible price of a commercial operation that netted $50,000,000 a year on the basis of his crossover appeal. His domestication for white audiences was definitively certified by a film in which he engaged in comical colloquies with familiar cartoon characters. As the late Arthur Ashe once pointed out, "advertisers want somebody who's politically neutered."

For the black athlete who refuses political neutering, the American sports world is a difficult venue in which to offer African-American analysis or promote an African-American agenda. The newspapers, networks and magazines that have a stake in the financial health of professional and collegiate sports operations tend to censor or downplay the existence of racial inequities or conflicts. While the addition of black sportswriters has led to more accurate coverage of racial situations, their more numerous white colleagues will frequently spin certain stories and just sit on others. When Latrell Sprewell choked his coach in 1997 it produced an orgy of publicity that played to every negative stereotype about black men. When a white NFL linebacker named Kevin Greene attacked his coach in 1998 during a game it was treated as a minor incident, because white anger and black anger are socially constructed in different ways. When *Sports Illustrated* published a roundtable discussion of the state of the NFL in 1999, neither black participant would accuse the league of systemic racism despite a reluctance to hire black coaches that has become obvious to the point of farce. . . .

The argument for integrated sport has always been that interracial teams and competitions promote better race relations. There is undoubtedly some truth to this claim, even if the social benefits can be difficult to confirm. The problem is that traditional ideas about the innocence and simplicity of the sports world have inflated its significance as an engine of social progress beyond anything we can confirm in an empirical way. In addition, the urgent need to find favorable signs and portents about where our racial predicament is heading has produced an untested theory of crossover effects that seizes on any black performer who can attract a white audience.

The critic Martha Bayles once pointed to "the simple fact that whites can genuinely appreciate black cultural styles without necessarily acquiring new sympathy or liking for their black fellow citizens." This is an arresting thought: precisely because we find it difficult to see black performances as unrelated to the forward or backward progress of race relations. "It is a powerful myth," Bayles notes, "shared by many performers, which decrees that widespread white acceptance of a black act can mean only one of two things: either the act is a coon show, or another breakthrough has occurred in American race relations.". . .

The Perpetuation of Racial Myths

The formation of social consciousness in Western societies has long included a racial typology that posits blacks and whites as polar opposites who differ both biologically and culturally. Only half a century ago discussion of such differences, both real and imagined, was accepted and quite uninhibited. As African Americans gained greater status and respect after the Second World War, the crudest and most ignorant assertions and speculations about racial differences were either discredited by more accurate information or entered into a state of suspended animation in which they could not be challenged by better informed ideas about race.

There is still a lot of such racial material floating around in peoples' heads, passed on from one generation to the next, because Western societies have done little to remove it. When, for example, the golfer Jack Nicklaus told an interviewer in 1994 that blacks were anatomically unsuited to play golf because they "have different muscles that react in different ways," he was invoking an eccentric racial biology of whose origins he was certainly unaware. In fact, the certainty with which he offered this fantasy was directly proportional to his indifference to where it had come from. It was simply and intuitively a fact about race. In a similar vein, I have heard people with no scientific training repeat mistaken dogmas about the bones and tendons of the "black" foot that supposedly give African-American sprinters their extra speed. These ideas appeared, and were discredited, during the 1930s. Yet there they were, like ancient dragonflies preserved in amber, floating out of brains that had somehow preserved them until the end of the twentieth century.

Racially integrated sport has preserved such racial folklore by giving the racial anthropology of the nineteenth century a new lease on life. The domination of various athletic events by specific ethnic or racial groups has promoted ideas about racial athletic aptitude throughout the twentieth century. Once upon a time the long-distance races were a specialty of the "stoic" Finns. Today it is darker-skinned stoics from North and East Africa. Nor is the racial folklore of sport a monopoly of the whites who have lost so much ground to fitter and darker competitors over the past generation. Black people absorb racial folklore with an efficiency that equals or exceeds that of whites, given their special emotional investment in athletic achievement and their awareness of the physical traumas endured by their ancestors. The notion that African Americans are the robust issue of breeding experiments has thus served the fantasy needs of blacks and whites alike. "We were simply bred for physical qualities," the Olympic champion sprinter Lee Evans said in 1971. Many other black athletes, as well as better-educated black men, have embraced the same eugenic myth. "Slavery," a black physician told the African-American medical association in 1962, "was the greatest biological experiment of all times. Slavery began with the trip to America, during which all of the weak ones were killed or thrown overboard or allowed to die. This was followed by the slave block, further selection and sales as desirable animals. From this point on, artificial mating occurred."

My research confirms what Franz Fanon pointed out in *Black Skin, White Masks* half a century ago, namely, that blacks and whites continue to ingest substantial quantities of a racial folklore that physicalizes black human beings while devaluing their minds. This demonstrates in turn the persisting influence of the nineteenth-century "law of compensation," which postulates an inverse relationship between brain and brawn. (The ubiquitous "dumb jock" stereotype is yet another version of this folk belief.) A long tradition of racist humor about black appetites for sex and food, the widespread popular belief in the eugenic breeding of slaves, the longevity of ideas about black immunities to pain and disease, the panracial belief in black athletic superiority—all of this confirms that black people have been identified with their bodies to an extraordinary degree.

The influence of such ideas on African Americans has never been studied in a systematic way. What we do know is that stereotypes of black athletic superiority are now firmly established as the most recent version of a racial folklore that has spread across the face of the earth over the past two centuries, and a corresponding belief in white athletic inferiority pervades popular thinking about racial difference. Such ideas probably do more than anything else in our public life to encourage the idea that blacks and whites are biologically different in meaningful ways. Conservative racial thinkers like Charles Murray and Dinesh D'Souza have declared that black athletic superiority is evidence of more profound racial differences, and there is no telling how many people, black and white, may agree with them.

Debunking the Athletic Black Stereotype

The potential consequences of regarding oneself as essentially or uniquely physical by nature would thus include particular doubts about one's intelligence, the value of getting an education, and the idea of learning for its own sake. This relates in turn to the growing interest in why the academic performance of socially advantaged black children continues to lag behind that of white children of comparable social status. "How do we explain the underproductivity of middle-class kids, of able and gifted minority youngsters who come out of situations where you would expect high achievement?" asks Edmund W. Gordon, a professor emeritus of psychology at Yale University and the co-chairman of the National Task Force on Minority High Achievement. "This is not something that a lot of people feel comfortable talking about."

Explaining this phenomenon will require cultural anthropological analysis of a very high order. I would also suggest that productive thinking about this problem need not be monopolized by the experts. Any parent who takes the time to reflect on the intellectual formation of his or her children will be able to identify some of the factors that are likely to promote the development of intellectual interests and self-confidence. Such factors do not include a sense that one's primary aptitude is physical self-expression. That is why one of our goals should be the abolition of a social universe in which African-American schoolchildren cannot believe that the black college students who come to mentor them are not athletes, since television has persuaded them that every black person is an athlete.

The Rise of Women's Sports

Nancy Struna

The following selection is adapted from an article that Nancy Struna wrote for the Women's Sports Foundation, a charitable educational organization dedicated to ensuring equal access to participation for all girls and women in sports. In the article, Struna traces the evolution of women's sports. Whereas in the first half of the eighteenth century women participated in a variety of sporting events, in the nineteenth century changing gender norms limited women to domestic and maternal activities. These gender roles were challenged repeatedly throughout the twentieth century. The watershed moment for women's sports came in 1972, when Title IX of the federal Educational Amendments Act mandated that education institutions receiving federal funds provide equal funding for men's and women's sports.

WOMEN'S EXPERIENCES IN THE SPORTING LIFE of the United States defy neat historical generalizations. In part this is because women never constituted a single group, and their behaviors and attitudes never conformed to a single general pattern. Women's roles also varied across time, connected as they were to the broader ideological and economic contexts. Sometimes women were active participants (in the modern sense) in a sport, while at other times they were behind-the-scenes producers or promoters.

Occasionally as well, women were consumers of sports, or

■

spectators, and there were times when perceptions of women's physical and moral "natures" affected sporting values, codes of conduct, rules, and even whether an activity was a sport or not. Indeed, the perceptions of women as the "weaker sex" helps to account for both the designation of bowling as an "amusement" when women engaged in it in the nineteenth century and the development of the divided court in basketball. Even today fans and the press persist in requiring basketball to be preceded by "women's." Women play women's basketball, while men simply play basketball.

Too often historians present women's sporting experiences as if they were rooted only in modern society and became increasingly more complex and common. The latter characterization is accurate for a particular period, such as the twentieth century, but across time, women's sporting experiences were episodic rather than evolutionary. At any given time they shaped, as much as they were shaped by, the wider web of social, economic, and political experiences. . . .

Changing Gender Roles

[In the mid–eighteenth century] middle- and upper-class women, especially those who either lived in or visited towns and cities, had access to the broadest range of sports and other recreations. In the South, white women who lived on plantations raced horses and went fox hunting. As did their northern contemporaries, they also attended balls, played cards, and attended the increasing array of physical culture exhibitions, which included race walking, tumbling and acrobatic displays, and equestrian shows.

The pursuit of active sports by women was not to persist, however. During the second half of the eighteenth century, a series of complex changes gradually altered gender roles and relations. Enlightenment ideology and the emergent capitalist economy combined to redefine women's place, to move them into the home and away from public activity, and to emphasize biological differences (from men) as grounds for keeping them there. In effect, the famous "doctrine of separate spheres" drew from the same movements that resulted in a new nation and a Declaration of Independence that proclaimed "all men are created equal." The phrase was not tongue-in-cheek; even before 1800, women were seen as morally superior but physically inferior to men. The characterization lasted for more than a century and a half.

The immediate impact of these changes was the movement of many, though by no means all, women off the tracks and fields and into the stands, or out of public view entirely, unless accompanied by men. The trend was especially pronounced in towns and cities among middle- and upper-class people whose lives were increasingly shaped by commercial and industrial tasks and rhythms and who came to believe that women's central role was to bear and nurture children and families. Slave and free women who continued to live and work on farms and plantations, as well as the increasing number who joined in the westward migration, did not experience the full weight of these changes in roles and lifestyles. . . . They remained visible producers and consumers of traditional sports and other displays of physical prowess.

During the first half of the nineteenth century, perceptions and real experiences suggested to some people that the health of middle- and upper-class women in urbanizing areas was declining. Educators, doctors, and writers of popular magazine articles responded with analyses and prescriptions for improving women's health, including calls for renewed physical exertion via exercises and games. The logic of the health literature was simple and straightforward: if women were to fulfill their roles as caretakers of families and national virtue, they needed to maintain their physical and mental health. People such as Catharine Beecher, Mary Lyons, and Diocletian Lewis thus argued for the physical education of women, started schools, and laid out regimens of calisthenics, domestic exercises (e.g., sweeping), and traditional activities such as walking and riding. The movement to return women to physically active pursuits had begun, albeit in their private, domestic sphere.

This would not, however, occur overnight. The urban areas that were home to many of the women targeted by the likes of Beecher and Lewis, as well as the economic activities that powered such areas, had reduced the social power of traditional sports and engendered an emerging new form, modern sports. Constructed by men for men, games such as baseball were becoming popular in eastern urban centers at mid-century. Other activities such as skating, croquet, and rowing were also modernizing, acquiring rules, specialized playing spaces, and an organizational base in clubs. Only gradually did women gain access to such forms. In the 1850s they did so primarily as spectators and moral guardians. Especially at baseball games, male promoters hoped that women would bring their perceived moral superiority to bear on the crowds and ensure social order. . . .

Middle- and upper-class urban women both found and made opportunities in public society during and after the Civil War that drew from their long-defined practices in their domestic sphere. Nursing and teaching were precisely such activities, but they were also ones that required additional training as well as sound constitutions. Not surprisingly, then, some women demanded and received access to colleges, where they did as their brothers did: they began to participate in some of the emerging modern sports whose social power was increasing in the aftermath of the Civil War and the technological and communication changes of the 1860s and 1870s. At private colleges such as Vassar in New York and Smith and Wellesley in Massachusetts, women students formed clubs to play baseball and, quickly, tennis, croquet, and archery. College administrators and faculty responded, initially to the influx of women and their own fears about the negative impact of intellectual work on women students, with requirements for medical examinations, exercise and gymnastics regimens, and the gradual absorption of women's sport clubs.

Outside of the colleges, post-war middle- and upper-class women were also moving to take advantage of the increasing array of modern sports. Local gymnasiums, armories turned into playing areas, and a host of clubs that formed as men and women sought new forms of community provided urban and townswomen with opportunities for a range of sports, from skating and rowing to trap shooting and tennis. Such activities continued to stretch the bounds of activity acceptable for and to women. They also quieted some of the fears held especially by the male-dominated medical profession about the negative effects that physical movement in sports might have on women's biology and reproductive functions.

An even more significant challenge to the nearly century-old ideology that placed women in the home and in subservience to men came in the form of a machine, the bicycle. Invented in Europe in the early 19th century, early versions of the bicycle had appeared in various forms and had become the object of short-lived fads through the 1860s. Then came the invention of the "ordinary" (one large and one small wheel) and, subsequently, the "safety" cycle, and the latter especially appealed to women. Bicycle riding, and even some racing, became popular, and the practice afforded women with a means of physical mobility and freedom that they had not known for generations, since the days when horse ownership was common and expected, even by women. Significantly, as well, the bicycle catalyzed dress reform. Bloomers and knickerbockers went on, and corsets came off. The day of the "new woman" was about to dawn.

The Age of Modern Sports

Historians have labeled the period from the 1890s to World War I as the Progressive era, largely because "progress" was the goal of contemporaries, especially members of the urban middle class. Achievement did not always match rhetoric, but many women did see their positions and the quality of their lives enhanced. Some urban working women, for instance, earned more pay and improved conditions, and perhaps not surprisingly, some of the industries that employed women organized, first, calisthenics or physical culture classes and then team sports to promote personal health and worker efficiency. Such programs became more widespread after the turn of the century, and by the 1920s individual companies and regional industries had multiple teams in sports such as basketball, bowling, tennis, baseball, volleyball, and eventually softball. Among the results were good advertising for the companies and competitive opportunities and even, on occasion, additional income for the athletes.

Another group of women whose lives came to incorporate opportunities for competitive sports were the upper-class women. In the 1870s and 1880s such women had joined clubs, social clubs, country clubs, and then sport-specific clubs, just as had their brothers and husbands. They also engaged in sports in colleges and, importantly, on their vacations or extended stays in Europe. By 1900 seven of these women competed in their first Olympics, in Paris, and despite the enduring opposition of the prime mover behind the modern Olympic Games, Baron Pierre de Coubertin, women consistently competed in the Games thereafter, albeit in small numbers and in socially acceptable sports such as tennis, archery, and even figure skating by 1924. . . .

After 1929 the Great Depression disrupted this sporting boom, but it did not end it entirely. In fact, the popularity of industrial sport likely peaked in the 1930s, and sports such as softball and bowling became extremely popular among women. Women's Olympic competition also gained more popular support, in part because of great performances by athletes such as Mildred "Babe" Didrikson and in part because support continued to diminish for the mythology of the negative physical and biological consequences of athletics for women. Significantly as well, women continued to enter nontraditional roles, a trend that became more pronounced as World War II began. After 1941 more and more women took jobs that had once belonged to the men who went abroad to fight. Even professional baseball opened its doors to women via the All-American Girls Baseball League financed by Philip Wrigley of chewing gum and Chicago Cubs fame.

Now famous in part because of the movie, *A League of Their Own*, the All-American Girls Baseball League began play in 1943 in mid-size cities in the Great Lakes region. The athletes were not, to be sure, the first professional women athletes in the United States. In the modern era that honor likely belongs to female distance walkers in the 1870s and 1880s and rodeo competitors in the twentieth century. Nor were they the only women professional athletes of the decade. After 1949 the Ladies Professional Golf Association organized, offering $15,000 in purse money spread over nine tournaments. Five years later, women golfers could earn $225,000 a year on the LPGA tour.

In the 1940s as well, an even more significant movement developed in African American colleges. Track and field teams were training at places such as Tuskegee Institute and Tennessee State, and these colleges would produce the athletes that would integrate U.S. women's Olympic teams and revolution-ize the contests and the records. By the early 1960s African-American athletes such as Wilma Rudolph ran record-pace after record-pace, opening doors for other black women and paving the way for Jackie Joyner-Kersee and Florence Griffith Joyner, among numerous others. Other sports such as bowling and tennis also integrated in the post–World War II years.

The Sixties Boom

A greater revolution in women's sports lay ahead. In the late 1960s the modern feminist movement, a youth culture, and other sources of social unrest unsettled both the nation as a whole and the sports world in particular. Billie Jean King defied international tennis tradition and authorities at Wimbledon in 1968, when she demanded an end to under-the-table payments; then she defeated another symbol of patriarchy, Bobby Riggs, on the court in 1973. In between King's two strikes for honesty and women, she helped organize the first of several early 1970s professional leagues for women, the Virginia Slims tennis tour.

King symbolized the commencement of contemporary women's revolution in sports, the realization of the image projected in the 1890s "new woman." Legislation, especially Title IX of the Educational Amendments Act of 1972, and the subsequent and ongoing litigation against unequal opportunities in institutions continued it, and probably had a greater impact on more women. Schools and colleges that accept federal funds now must provide athletic opportunities for women proportional to the number of women they enroll, and few women are unaffected.

There has been a dynamic and continuing growth of women's sports since the late 1960s. Triathlons, marathons, soccer, aerobics, weightlifting, rugby, skiing, two professional basketball leagues (although one folded in late 1998), athletic clubs, and even cheerleading are among the many sports available to women, none of which existed a century ago and few of which existed a generation earlier. What remains unknown is the full impact of the generation of women who are now maturing and who grew up with opportunities that their mothers and grandmothers never dreamed of.

Femininity and Feminism in the WNBA

Sarah Banet-Weiser

Sarah Banet-Weiser teaches at the Annenberg School for Communication at the University of Southern California. In the following selection, she discusses the challenge that female athletes face in gaining respect as competitors while still maintaining the qualities traditionally associated with femininity, such as motherhood, beauty, and morality. Banet-Weiser focuses on how players in the Women's National Basketball Association (WNBA) gained popularity for meeting this challenge. Banet-Weiser suggests that by combining athleticism and competitiveness with the traditional notions of femininity, WNBA athletes are offering a new conception of femininity and serving as powerful role models for young girls.

"THE WOMEN HAVE ARRIVED!" THE WNBA AD reads, implicitly arguing that there is, in fact, a place for a professional women's basketball league. . . .

The American public's fascination with female athletes has almost always centered on individual athletes: tennis players, professional golfers, figure skaters, and gymnasts. These sports demonstrate the agility and elegance "natural" to women and, although athleticism is clearly a major aspect of these sports, the individual stars are known, culturally at least, more for their "feminine" attributes: self-sacrifice, glamour, grace. Indeed, the public recognition of individual female athletes attends much

■

Sarah Banet-Weiser, "Hoop Dreams: Professional Basketball and the Politics of Race and Gender," *Journal of Sport and Social Issues*, vol. 23, November 1999, pp. 403–20.

more to their feminine beauty and objectified status as particular kinds of commodities than to their athletic skill. And, if individual women athletes are not naturalized as sexual, feminine beings, it is usually because they are not, in fact, women at all, but rather little girls. In the last decade, sports such as tennis, figure skating, and gymnastics can hardly be called women's sports: Tara Lipinski won the Olympic gold medal in figure skating when she was 14 years old, there was not a single individual more than 20 years old on the recent American Olympic team of female gymnasts, and tennis superstar Martina Hingis became famous at 17 years old. But the WNBA is not only a team sport, it is a team sport for women: The players are required to complete their college eligibility or be 21 years old. Hence, they can acquire their status as role models for little girls—an important feature of professional team sports in the United States—precisely because, unlike Tara Lipinski or Kerry Strugg, they are not little girls. In fact, it is the maturity of the players that is often lauded in the press. The focus on maturity accomplishes at least two different things. First, it establishes the players as experienced professionals, not little girls who will, simply because of physical development, grow too large at any moment to be a superstar gymnast or ice skater. It also establishes the WNBA players as different from the NBA players. The maturity of the WNBA is in direct contrast to the "immaturity" of the NBA.

But because the masculinist assumptions of team sports challenge the individualist and moralist ideology that constructs sports such as figure skating and gymnastics, the women athletes in the WNBA have had to manage a contradictory set of cultural images. Strategies are needed to reassure fans that although they are not dancing gracefully over the ice in designer outfits, professional female basketball players are, in fact, feminine beings. And while for some, the WNBA is a shining example of the transcendence of gender in professional sports, a place where finally, gender does not "matter," it is just as clear that gender matters tremendously. . . .

Fashionable Players: WNBA and Glamour

The traditional trappings of femininity—fashion, motherhood, beauty, morality—characterize the players of the WNBA. For example, on the official Website of the WNBA, alongside features that list game schedules, highlights from previous games, and new sponsorship partners, there is a section called "WNBA Unveils Uniform." This section claims that the WNBA "injects fresh perspective into the creation of its basketball uniforms," and there is information about the decisions made for the official WNBA uniforms: Should they wear dresses? Tunics over shorts? Unitards? Or "skorts" (skirts/shorts)? There is also detailed information about the materials and colors used for the final choice of uniforms (which, incidentally, was shirts and shorts). Finally, there is a section where fans can vote on their favorite uniform, with pictures of both the home and away uniforms. Clearly, this particular section of the Website contributes to a dominant ideology that women are overly concerned with clothing and fashion. There is no comparable section on the Website of the NBA, and, although it is not surprising, the presence of this feature tells us something about the various ways in which the players and the institution of the WNBA function to shore up dominant notions and ideologies about the construction of womanhood. Given the threat that is posed by paying women to play basketball and thus recognizing them as professionals, naturalizing them as "true women" is a predictable strategy.

The fact that some of the WNBA players also model is something that is emphasized by reporters. The modeling career of Lisa Leslie, a player for the Los Angeles Sparks, is the consistent focus of the articles that feature her [as this excerpt from a 1996 *Women's Sport and Fitness* article demonstrates]:

> The worlds of hoops and haute couture seem galaxies apart to most people. Not Lisa Leslie. All poise and confidence, the Olympic gold medalist and aspiring supermodel is equally comfortable dribbling down the lane in a sweaty fury and breezing down the runway in four-inch heels and an Armani evening gown.

It is clear that it is absolutely crucial for Leslie to be "equally" comfortable in either the athlete or model mode—it is precisely this easy movement between the two that helps legitimate her status as a star athlete. As Leslie herself puts it [in a July 1997 *Sport* article], "That's what I call my Wonder

Woman Theory. . . . When I'm playing, I'll sweat and talk trash. However, off the court, I'm lipstick, heels, and short skirts. I'm very feminine, mild-mannered, and sensitive." The rest of the article is quite bald-faced about this particular strategy, calling the "sudden" fact that "women's hoops are vogue, chic, and feminine" as "all part of the plan." This is clearly about establishing the WNBA players' commitment to being feminine, and an explicit argument against the history of female athletes, who were so often criticized for their distinctly unfeminine qualities, such as muscularity and athletic skill. . . .

Compulsory Heterosexuality and the WNBA

Indeed, the threat of women participating in the sporting world is by no means a new one. Susan Cahn has argued that the stereotype of the mannish lesbian athlete has worked to shape not only female competitors themselves, but also sports organizations, funding sources, and the overall popularity of women's sports. The most common strategy employed by athletic organizations to overcome this stereotype is to reassure audiences and fans that women involved in sports are indeed "women"— meaning, of course, that they are heterosexual. As Cahn points out, "The lesbian stereotype exert[s] pressure on athletes to demonstrate their femininity and heterosexuality, viewed as one and the same." Not surprisingly, it is in those sports that most resemble masculinized athletics (for example, softball or hockey), and those that have the greatest need to attract a paying audience, that the fear of and anxiety over lesbianism are most prominent. Because these sports are culturally defined as masculine, and because there is an easy cultural slippage between "masculine women" and lesbian identity, strategies are needed by the players to redefine and recast the sport as feminine or womanly. For example, "flex appeal" is translated as "sex appeal" in the context of female body building, female tennis players are often depicted as "playing for" their love interest in the stands, and female professional basketball players are shown as fashion models and mothers. . . .

Balancing Baby with Basketball

A successful strategy to reassure fans of the players' heterosexuality has been to focus on maternity. When WNBA star

Sheryl Swoopes of the Houston Comets became pregnant the first season of the league, it proved to be a great advantage to her as a player, as well as a golden marketing opportunity for the league. When asked about Swoopes, Rick Welts [chief marketing officer for the NBA and WNBA] said, "We embrace maternity." Swoopes's pregnancy became a press bonanza, with soft news stories about maternity in general, balancing baby with basketball, and the generous sacrifice of Swoopes's husband, Eric Jackson, to stay home with the baby. Rosie O'Donnell, an extremely public WNBA fan, is exuberant in her praise of Swoopes, explicitly because of her maternity:

> People go to NBA games and they can figure out pretty fast that Michael Jordan is the most valuable player because he's the best. WNBA fans don't think that way. Our MVP was Sheryl Swoopes, not because she led the league in scoring or acrobatics, but because she had a baby and six weeks later, she was back on the court playing basketball . . . . [She continues] Sheryl gets ready to go in the game and every mom in the crowd stands up and cheers: "Hey Sheryl! Go girl! Can you believe how good she looks! She had a baby! Go Sheryl! You still nursing? Sheryl, you look great!"

When Swoopes plays, the camera continually returns to shots of the sideline, where the baby and father watch the game. . . .

Establishing the WNBA as a sporting event for the family is an important discursive move. The league is often lauded as a "hoop dream come true for millions of American girls," and it is explicitly marketed as a sport the whole family can watch together. Moreover, the long-held dominant ideology that women are "morally superior" to men finds its way to the WNBA in the way that the women athletes are seen as less corrupted, whether by power or money, than NBA athletes. The players of the WNBA often talk about their teams as their family; as Cynthia Cooper of the Houston Comets said, "Families are very, very important to me, both my own family and the family that I have on the court, because we did become a family during the season." In turn, the wholesome quality of the WNBA is both constituted and bolstered by the increasing public disapproval of bad-boy behavior in the NBA. As one columnist [C. Kallam] put it,

For women's basketball to become a major sport in America, as opposed to a profitable one like arena football, something is going to have to be offered other than just pure skill. That something should be, and in fact will have to be, a different attitude, a purer sense of the sport, than the men deliver.

This "different attitude" resides in the bodies of the female players, indeed, is the bodies of the players, bodies that are more moral, more pure, less likely to succumb to temptation, and less corrupt than male bodies. Simply, the bodies of the WNBA players are the "purer sense of the sport." This comparison with professional male basketball players serves a particular purpose: The "moral" feminine bodies of the WNBA players perform the cultural work of restabilizing the racial bodies of NBA players. In other words, media portrayals of the defiant, "bad" behavior of professional male basketball players situates the WNBA as a positive alternative, a sport that emphasizes a kind of feminine behavior and attitude that contains the unruliness of the NBA. The discourse of the family and maternity play into this dual construction, where the family-oriented players of the WNBA offer wholesome good fun and healthy competition to their fans, as opposed to the lone mavericks of the NBA, seemingly out only for themselves and their own personal glory.

Showing Some Respect

Although, clearly, the feminine body of the WNBA player is naturalized through a variety of discourses and strategies, it is also the case that the players are not objectified in the way that women's bodies have been objectified traditionally. They are constantly referred to in the press as "mature women," and the play itself shapes the bodies of the players as active subjects rather than passive objects, team players rather than prima donnas. Ann Meyers, a former All-American basketball player and currently a coach, has pointed out,

> Basketball is basketball, regardless of gender, race, or age.
> . . . The women's edge is they do the fundamentals. It's a
> great game. The men's game has gotten out of hand a little
> bit. They carry the ball, they travel. They've gotten away

from fundamentals. The taunting, the fights, the trash talking. I don't think there's any place for it in the game.

. . . Moreover, the purity of the WNBA is recognized through the gratitude of the players. Before the WNBA and the American Basketball League (ABL) were established, the only place where women could play professional basketball was overseas. The players of the WNBA were grateful to have a professional organization in the United States, and they consistently demonstrate this gratitude to their fans. Traditionally, gratitude, like self-sacrifice, has been a characteristic of femininity. . . .

Despite the gestures toward conformity displayed by WNBA athletes, the league does offer new potentials and conditions for shifting dominant understandings of femininity. Journalist Robyn Marks writes about the WNBA:

> The new-age prototype for Cosmo Woman has (finally!) turned the page from bikiniclad babes with big, er, smiles to women in baggy shorts, ponytails, and killer jump shots. Meet the new millennium of supermodels, led by Lisa Leslie, Rebecca Lobo, and Sheryl Swoopes. Hope you're buying, 'cause the WNBA is definitely selling.

This article continues to claim that the WNBA is "attempting to change the public perception of what femininity really is"—a tall order, clearly, but one that an all-female, professional team sports league may have a better shot at than, say, academics or Madonna. [Such articles suggest] that the American public is eager for strong, aggressive, competitive, female role models. The idea of modeling for girls and young women has been both a lucrative marketing strategy and, it seems, a realistic goal for the WNBA players. For example, a Nike television advertisement shown on Lifetime in August 1998 depicts Cynthia Cooper of the Houston Comets, who simply says to the camera:

> We get out in the malls and we're laughing and joking and I actually took a picture with the first person—she hasn't sent it to me yet—with the first little girl that I saw with my jersey. It was awesome. It was awesome. I wanted to cry. She came up to me and she said, "Would you please sign my autograph?" I said, "Can I take a picture with you, pleeeaasse?" It was great. It was amazing.

The ad ends with a stylized black and white photograph of Cooper, with the words "I can inspire" merging with the words "I can aspire."

This ad is typical for Nike, a company that has found role modeling for young girls to be an emotive and profitable strategy. Indeed, it is promising that girls and young women can witness a public validation of women who do not quite fit normative standards of femininity—that there is, in short, a public role model for young girls that looks and acts different from the current Miss America.

As "girl culture" emerges as an interesting and necessary site for scholarly study, it seems the WNBA is a perfect subject of inquiry. . . . The sheer physicality of the sport—a physicality that is so visually different from the way women's bodies are traditionally imaged and imagined—makes it a place where one can conceptualize new conditions of possibility for definitions of the feminine.

Thus, despite the various ways in which the WNBA normalizes conventional notions of femininity, the league, and the politics of gender that both surround and shape it, present an opportunity for a disruption of these conventions. The WNBA has already been hailed as a cultural realm that offers something different for both girls and women. The hip 1990s adage, "Girl Power," has been applied to the WNBA, and although this slogan has a clear transparency to it (after all, it was coined by The Spice Girls) the association of power with girls, whatever the source, deserves at least some critical attention. The major sponsors of the WNBA, Nike and Reebok, have adopted explicit liberal feminist rhetoric in their advertisements, and although obviously this language is a lucrative avenue for selling products, it nonetheless shapes the dominant construction of women athletes. Clearly, this last decade of the 20th century marks a moment where dominant norms of gender and race are negotiated in interesting and complex ways, and professional basketball—both the NBA and the WNBA—are situated at the center of these negotiations.

The Changing Face of Diversity in Sports

Richard E. Lapchick

Richard E. Lapchick is the founder and director of Northeastern University's Center for the Study of Sport in Society (CSSS) and the author of *Smashing Barriers: Race and Sport in the New Millennium,* from which the following article is excerpted. In it, Lapchick discusses the CSSS's 2001 *Racial and Gender Report Card.* According to the report card, the proportion of blacks playing in the major pro sports leagues has decreased, while the proportion of Latinos and other minorities has increased. However, women and minorities are still underrepresented in management positions. Lapchick also discusses a number of specific diversity issues in sports, including the controversy over Native American team names, the success of Tiger Woods and Venus and Serena Williams, and the growing acceptance of black quarterbacks in the NFL.

FIFTY YEARS HAVE PASSED SINCE MY DAD [JOE Lapchick] helped integrate the National Basketball Association as coach of the Knicks. That was three years after Jackie Robinson blazed a much harder trail as the first black player in Major League Baseball. Robinson had two dreams—the integration of the players and the integration of management. The first seems complete. The integration of blacks, Latinos, and

■

Richard E. Lapchick, *Smashing Barriers: Race and Sport in the New Millennium.* Lanham, MD: Madison Books, 2001. Copyright © 1991 by Richard E. Lapchick. Reproduced by permission.

international players onto American professional and college teams is nothing short of remarkable. The second part of Robinson's dream is far from complete.

Until very recently, discussions on the issue of diversity in sport focused almost exclusively on black and white players, but sport in America is no longer a snapshot of black and white. Diversity is being redefined for the new millennium.

In November, 1999, Northeastern University's Center for the Study of Sport in Society released its tenth annual report regarding the racial composition of players, coaches, and key administrators in the NBA, the WNBA, the NFL, Major League Baseball, the NHL, Major League Soccer, and college sport. The report, long known as the *Racial Report Card*, was

Table 1. African American Players in Professional and College Sport (from 2001 *Racial and Gender Report Card*)

League	Year	Percentage of African Americans
National Basketball Association	2000–01	78%
Women's Nat. Basketball Assoc.	2000	63%
National Football League	2000	67%
Major League Baseball	2000	13%
National Hockey League	1999–2000	2%
Major League Soccer	2000	16%
NCAA Basketball	1998–1999	56%
NCAA Football	1998–1999	46%
NCAA Baseball	1998–1999	2%
Other NCAA Division I sports	1998–1999	25%

renamed the *Racial and Gender Report Card*. The data on African American participation appears [in Table 1]. Despite the widely held perception that the number of black athletes continues to soar in the major sports, these tables reinforce the conclusion that racial diversity in sport will no longer be only about black and white.

Since the early 1990s, the percentage of black players decreased in all professional sports as well as at the Division I collegiate level. The percentage of black players in Major League Baseball hit a ten-year low point in 2000. In Division I men's college basketball and baseball, the percentage of black student-athletes was at the lowest level since 1991–92, while the total percentage of black student-athletes playing Division I sports dropped from 25.2 percent in 1991–92 to 25 percent in 1996–97.

For the most part, these declining numbers have remained stable or, in some cases, decreased further. As of November 2000, blacks made up 78 percent of the players in the NBA, 63 percent in the Women's National Basketball Association, 67 percent in the National Football League, 13 percent in Major League Baseball, 56 percent in college basketball, and 46 percent in college football.

On the other hand, the percent of Latino players in MLB in 2000 reached an all-time high of 26 percent, and that number is climbing. Their presence continues to grow in Major League Soccer. In Division I college sport the total number of players of color reached 32.1 percent of all student-athletes, due in large part to the increase in the number of Latino, Asian, and Native American student-athletes.

In the 2000 WNBA season, 34 percent of the players were white, 63 percent were black, and 3 percent were Latino. In the 2000 NHL season, 2 percent of the players were black. There were also three Asian players, and six players from other minorities. In the 2000 Major League Soccer season, 63 percent of the players were white, 16 percent were black, 21 percent were Latino, and 1 percent were Asian American.

International players control 11 percent of the slots for players in the NBA, 18 percent in the WNBA, 3 percent in the NFL, 12 percent in MLB (excluding American-born players of Latino descent), 25 percent in MLS, and 6 percent in college sports.

The NBA consistently holds the best record for opportunities for people of color and women in management positions. Among the new men's leagues covered for the first time in the 1999 *Racial and Gender Report Card*, Major League Soccer had the best record for racial diversity and the NHL had the best record for opportunities for women. In light of the small number of NHL players who are racial minorities, the NHL had a better than expected record on racial diversity, especially in the league office. By comparison, the colleges and universities had the poorest record of all once again.

Off the playing fields and courts, Jackie Robinson's second dream remains unfulfilled. The 1999 *Racial and Gender Report Card* shows that while hiring practices in sport have improved for people of color and women, there is clearly room for progress in all sports. Yet, according to the Federal Glass Ceiling Commission Report (FGCR), pro sport was far ahead of society in these matters. Whereas affirmative action programs have been under siege in many states, both college and pro sports assert that their goal is to embrace affirmative action.

One of the most important findings of the RGRC was that

Table 2. International Players in Professional Sports (from 2001 *Racial and Gender Report Card*)

League	Year	Percentage of International Players
National Basketball Association	1999–2000	11%
Women's Nat. Basketball Assoc.	2000	18%
National Football League	2000	3%
Major League Baseball	2000	12%
National Hockey League	1999–2000	26%
Major League Soccer	2000	25%

the growth of opportunities for women continued to exceed those for people of color by significant numbers for professional off-the-field positions in both college and professional sports. However, many of the jobs held by women indicated that there is still a gendered division of labor in sport. Despite important gains, women are overrepresented in support staff positions and are underrepresented, aside from in the NBA, in senior management.

When compared with the league offices in the NFL and MLB, the NBA had the highest percentage of employees of color (22 percent) and female employees (45 percent). The total percentage of minorities in the NBA league office was down only slightly from 30 percent in 1997 to 29 percent, while in the NFL league office the total percentage of minorities was 23 percent, up slightly from 1997. At the NFL league office, people of color held 21 percent of professional posts and women held 26 percent.

Since 1997 there has been a 1 percent increase in the number of black employees and a 4 percent increase in the total number of minorities at the executive and department head level in Major League Baseball in central offices. Overall, minorities make up 26 percent of all MLB personnel. However, the percentage of women represented at the executive and department head level dropped 9 percent from 1997.

In the NHL in 1999, 19 percent of the professional staff was made up of people of color and 41 percent were women. At the MLS league office, the professional staff was 81 percent white, 17 percent Latino, 2 percent Asian, and 47 percent female.

Val Ackerman, president of the WNBA, is the only woman to head a major professional sports league. In 1999, 31 percent of WNBA league office employees were minorities. Women made up 69 percent of the total staff at the office. In addition, 31 percent of the WNBA head coaches were black, of which 13 percent were black women. Though many staff members of the WNBA's central offices are shared with the NBA, all data referred to here are for all personnel employed only by the WNBA.

There were no black or Latino majority owners in the NBA, the NFL, the NHL, the WNBA, Major League Soccer, or Major League Baseball. There was one Asian majority owner in MLS and one in the NHL. Three majority owners were women: two in the NFL and one in MLB.

The NBA, the NHL, and MLS all had people of color as team presidents or chief executive officers (CEOs). However, the NFL and MLB did not report any people of color holding the positions of board chairs, presidents, or CEOs. Marge Schott was once the only female president/CEO in MLB, then heading-up the Cincinnati Reds. In August 1998, Wendy Selig-Prieb assumed that role with the Milwaukee Brewers.

As of May 2001, the three major professional sports leagues combined reported 19 head coaches and managers who were persons of color, an increase of 6 from 1999 and a new all-time high. Major League Soccer had two Latino head coaches. At the start of the 2000–01 NHL season, persons of color held none of the head coaching positions.

The number of people of color in the role of the "principal in charge of day to day operations," positions such as general manager or director of player personnel, also increased by June 2001. There were six African American general managers in the NBA, 4 in the NFL and one in MLB where the Chicago White Sox had baseball's only black general manager. In the 2000–2001 NHL season, as well as Major League Soccer's 2000 season, no persons of color held a similar position. Lynne Meterparel, general manager of the San Jose Clash, was the only female general manager in men's professional sports. Of the five general managers in the WNBA, three were women and one was African American. . . .

Native American Names and Mascots in Sport

In one day, Hank Aaron did more for the campaign to ban Native American team names and mascots than has been accomplished in the thirty-plus years that the campaign has been active. As fans gathered for the 2000 All-Star Classic in Atlanta, Aaron couldn't resist the platform that throwing out the first pitch gave him. He talked to the media about race and sport. This was not new for the man who had his own personal triumph of breaking Babe Ruth's career home run record marred by innumerable death threats and a barrage of hate mail. What was new was his statement that if the team name that he had worn on his chest for decades was hurtful to many Native

Americans, then it should be changed. He instantly became the most prominent athlete to take that position publicly.

Hank Aaron is a high ranking executive for the Atlanta Braves. Ted Turner, the team owner and a well-known philanthropist who has given generously for Goodwill Games designed to increase understanding between people of different nationalities, never questioned the appropriateness of his team's name. To a certain extent I can understand his blindness, because in my youth I shared it.

I played freshman basketball for the St. John's Redmen. My father coached those Redmen for twenty years, and was affectionately called "the Big Indian." He never had reason to question the nickname or the wooden Indian mascot and neither did I until an incident that happened late one evening in 1969 at Mama Leone's Restaurant near the old Madison Square Garden. Whenever we were there to eat after a game, people would come up to my father to greet him or ask for an autograph. This night was no different until an older man who appeared to be in his late sixties, like my father, asked if he could join us.

The man told my father how much he admired him as a coach and as someone who helped to integrate basketball. We smiled until he added that these things made it particularly embarrassing that my father coached a team called the Redmen and was called "the Big Indian." The man was a Native American.

That was the first time that we had ever thought about what the Redmen represented. We began to conjure up memories of headlines, "Redmen on the Warpath" and "Redmen Scalp Braves [Bradley University]." The Braves even "hung the Redmen" once. The question of the appropriateness of the team name continued to haunt the school for another twenty years until St. John's, like other universities, came to understand the offense and rid itself of a name and symbols representing Native American stereotypes.

However, in 2001, more than forty colleges and universities and five professional teams, including the Braves, retain Native American names and symbols. Would we think of calling teams the "Chicago Caucasians," the "Buffalo Blacks," or the "San Diego Jews"? Could you imagine people mocking

African-Americans in blackface at a game? Yet go to a game where there is a team with an Indian name and you will see fans with war paint on their faces. Is this not the equivalent of blackface? Although the thought of changing tradition is often painful, the sting of racism is even more painful.

Supporters of maintaining the team names and mascots that are potentially offensive to Native Americans generally claim that their use furthers our appreciation of Native American culture. They say that names are meant positively, that to be called a "Brave" is a compliment. There are even Native Americans who don't challenge that view. Nonetheless, most Native Americans believe that campuses where Indian names and mascots are used can be hostile learning environments not only for Native American students, but also for all students of color and for all students who care about stopping the spread of racism.

Concerned students, faculty and administrators point out that most campuses where Native American symbols prevail lack a Native American studies department and these schools do not make a serious attempt to recruit Native American students and faculty. The fact that history has ignored the incredible pain inflicted on Native Americans does not excuse colleges and universities from responding to potential pain inflicted by degrading mascots.

Along with all people of color and women who fight for their rights, more voices must be raised to make people who look like me become uncomfortable, just as that Native American man made my father and me uncomfortable in Mama Leone's in 1969. Like Hank Aaron did before the All-Star game.

In June 2000 I spoke against the continued use of Native American team names and mascots at the Sovereignty Symposium in Tulsa, Oklahoma. This symposium is an annual gathering of Native American leaders to discuss issues of their sovereignty—how to protect it where it is intact and how to reclaim it where it has been stolen. The use of Native American names and mascots for sports teams is one of the issues Native Americans believe is a breach of their sovereignty. Native Americans believe that all people live within the one circle of humanity, no matter what the color of their skin. Sports teams should honor that circle.

New Barriers Falling: Tennis and Golf Open Up

Golf and tennis have been the whitest of our sports, largely reserved for the wealthy and for those living in the suburbs. Can the play of Tiger Woods and Venus and Serena Williams change that? . . .

It may sound incredible to most, but according to two recent studies, The ESPN-Chilton study and the Neilsen Media Research study, African-Americans are the most avid tennis fans of any racial group. There was a great deal of excitement surrounding the women in the 2000 U.S. Open. Much of it emanated from an anticipated final that was not to be between the African American Williams sisters, Serena and Venus. Not long ago having an African American man or woman in the final was incredibly unlikely. Yet in 1999, Serena won it all. The 2000 Open belonged to Venus.

I have followed the USTA for nearly thirty years. Based on my own early contact, I would never have predicted the diverse makeup of today's fans. The USTA has been transformed from an organization that stood for exclusion to one that has moved toward inclusion. Tennis' grasses have been turning into welcoming places for the masses.

With the spectacular play of the Williams sisters, tennis again has stars of color. Tennis has had some recent African American stars and role models like Zina Garrison and Mali Vai Washington, but the Williams sisters have been incredible catalysts. Their arrival peaked even more interest in tennis in the African American community. In 1999, 11 percent of African-Americans called themselves avid tennis fans, a 36 percent increase over the results of a poll taken two years earlier. This is nearly twice the 5.7 percent of whites that identified themselves as tennis fans. Tennis is the fourth most popular sport among African-Americans after the NFL (39 percent), the NBA (37.4 percent), and MLB (18.2 percent). It is the seventh most popular sport among whites after the NFL (29 percent), MLB (18.9 percent), the NBA (15.4 percent), motor sports (12 percent), golf (9 percent), and the NHL (8 percent).

Urban youth tennis programs have been tremendously helpful in increasing tennis' popularity. By providing opportunities for children of color to learn the game, many white USTA officials, coaches, and players are showing these children that there is opportunity open to them in sport. Even more, such opportunities further diversity among athletes and support for all players irrespective of color. Targeting urban areas to spread the benefits of sport can help heal some of America's racial wounds and can help give children a vision of a better future. . . .

I cheered when I saw Tiger Woods' first television commercial in which he criticized restrictive golf courses that prohibited many people of color from playing there. However, Tiger was burned by the press for what I saw as his courage. Between 1998 and 1999 golf received a 14 percent boost in its African American fan base from Woods' play. Golf officials have taken note and have marketed Tiger with unprecedented success. He is making huge money for his sport. Maybe the same will happen for Serena [and] Venus. Maybe their collective successes will really open the floodgates, not just for more players who look like them, but also for an openness of attitude that will celebrate their individualism, creativity, courage, and honesty. . . .

It seemed like I couldn't read a newspaper or sports magazine for months in 1999 without seeing the faces of five great quarterbacks slotted to go high in the 1999 NFL draft. Of the five quarterbacks chosen among the first twelve picks, three— Syracuse's Donovan McNabb, Oregon's Akili Smith, and Central Florida's Daunte Culpepper—were black. I took more than twenty-five calls from writers asking me what I thought the significance of this was.

I knew that only three black quarterbacks had been drafted in the first round in the history of the NFL draft. In 1999, three black players were chosen in the first round of the draft. Will the stereotype of the smart, heroic, white quarterback leading the team be shattered forever? Does this mean that we have come a very long way on the issue of race in the NFL and in professional sports in general?

Considering how many calls I received, I smiled at several draft analysts who asserted that no one was really paying attention to color and that teams were simply selecting the best available talent. I agree with the latter part of the equation. Teams who want to win are finally picking the best players. I was happy to read Daunte Culpepper's comment, "Luckily for me, I wasn't faced with those issues. Maybe it doesn't matter that we're black quarterbacks as much as we are good quarterbacks." I think Daunte is right in this case. But we must not overstate the significance of this draft. Race does matter in the NFL and in the other major professional sports.

In the 1998 season of the NFL, the positions of quarterback, wide receiver, corner back, and safety were unevenly distributed among the races. At 91 percent, whites continued to dominate the position of quarterback, considered to be football's thinking and control position. White players also accounted for 83 percent of the players at center, considered by many to be football's second control position. On the other hand, blacks made up 92 percent of wide receivers, 87 percent of running backs, 99 percent of cornerbacks, and 99 percent of safeties, positions where speed and reactive ability are considered essential. The quarterback and center positions require more brains while the others reflect more brawn. These numbers imply that the brainy positions are occupied by whites while the brawny ones go to African-Americans. Given these percentages, the significant number of black quarterbacks drafted in the first round of the 1999 draft is notable.

Positional stacking seems to exist in Major League Baseball as well. In the 1998 season only 5 percent of pitchers and 4 percent of catchers were black. These two positions are considered to be baseball's thinking and control positions. Most black players remained in the outfield, where speed and reactive ability are prized. Blacks make up only 13 percent of baseball's players, but have held more than 45 percent of the outfield posts over the last two decades.

The 1999 NFL draft could well be a sign that positional segregation will become a thing of the past in professional football. McNabb and Culpepper have had great starts in their NFL careers. I hope they will get other opportunities if their successes are temporarily derailed at some point. There have been too many cases where black athletes who don't star in the game aren't kept around as bench players. Black quarterbacks throughout NFL history have rarely joined second or third string players in waiting for another chance. Several have been asked to play other positions. I hope that McNabb, Smith, and Culpepper will enjoy a very different future and inspire further change.

EXAMINING *POP* CULTURE

Professional Sports as Show Business and Big Business

The Marketing of Pro Sports

David Whitson

In the article below, David Whitson, a professor of Canadian studies at the University of Alberta, examines how the media and professional leagues work to make pro sports as popular and as profitable as possible. Coverage of sports as news, for example, allows the media to report on sports-related events virtually all the time, even when games are not occurring, and national coverage of sporting events enables teams to develop national, rather than local or regional, fan bases. The sports media also work to build up sports celebrities that will draw more fans, and using these athletes in advertisements enables corporate sponsors to associate their brand names with athletic success. With all the marketing avenues available to the pro sports industry and its associated media, Whitson concludes, the potential revenues are almost unlimited.

IT WAS OBSERVED SOME YEARS AGO BY [REsearcher P.] Bourdieu (1978) that the professionalization of popular sports, like that of "folk" music, simply returns to ordinary people, as paying spectators, commodified versions of practices with which they had once entertained themselves. Early professional sport was not yet commodified in all the ways we know today, if by commodification we mean production for the primary purpose of making a profit. However, the production and staging of sport as commercial entertainment led to the emergence of entrepreneurial structures and prac-

■

tices that would slowly transform the relationships between sporting teams and the communities they ostensibly "represent." Among the most important early developments were the ownership of teams by private entrepreneurs, the movement of both teams and players to larger cities where there were higher profits and salaries to be made, and the formation of combines of team operators (i.e., leagues) who achieved national market domination (and labor market domination) within their particular sports. . . .

In the early days of spectator sport, teams were largely composed of local men, and operated under the auspices of "clubs" that acted as organizers of ethnic, class, or town affiliations. Together, these phenomena contributed to a popular sense that teams were community institutions, and that their performance reflected the character of the communities they represented. Sporting contests between rival communities were full of social symbolism, and local "derbies" served as occasions for public rehearsals of the class, ethnic and religious identities that structured life in these rapidly industrializing societies. In these circumstances, cheering for one's "home" team was taken for granted, and most fans identified with the fortunes of their local team. However, as the potential for making money from the staging of sporting entertainment became clearer, and as cities themselves grew and changed, these community associations and meanings would be abraded and transformed by the logic of the marketplace. By the late twentieth century, although professional sports operators routinely appeal to civic (and national) sentiments when it suits their commercial purposes, the languages of communal traditions and loyalties are increasingly supplanted by corporate images and by the discourse of consumer choice. . . .

Media Coverage of Pro Sports

A key factor in building interest in professional sports was simply the normalization of the practice of reporting sports results as news. With the development of the sports sections and sportscasts that became regular features of the daily news, sport would stay "in the news" all week, even when there was no action on the field. Trade gossip, injury reports, pregame hype and postgame analysis all sustained interest in professional sports between events, and helped to establish the serial sagas of the sporting seasons as a familiar feature of North American popular life. . . .

One of the most effective forms of sports coverage for building audiences was human interest stories that invited identifications with the participants (favorite players, managers, rookies, etc.). Games were prefigured as contests between individuals, and readers were invited to identify with their hopes and plans—and afterwards, to share in the joys of victory and agonies of defeat. For those players who acquired reputations for producing the goods in decisive situations—whether home runs, goals, or touchdowns—their feats became legendary, and the men themselves were constructed as larger than life characters. Such attention has turned figures from Babe Ruth to Wayne Gretzky into household names, and along with similar "star-making" publicity in the film and music industries, it has helped create the phenomenon of the celebrity entertainer. Famous names were shown to promote interest in the sports events or films they were part of, and also to help sell the products they endorsed. Thus, it was not long before the media and entertainment industries recognized their common stake in the manufacture of "names" for a public demonstrably fascinated by stardom. . . .

By the late 1930s it was possible to see in outline what would become the ubiquitous place of professional sport in North American popular culture. It is important to recognize that it was the development of newspaper chains and radio networks that became, in effect, national information systems, that facilitated the development of common knowledge and interests among geographically dispersed regions. Yet the fact that the emergence of national media in America was driven by the interests of advertisers in reaching national audiences also meant that the lines between news, entertainment, and advertising would be constantly blurred. This would help to make the place of both professional sport and its sponsors in the fun-oriented consumer culture that was part of the promise of "America" in the interwar period, and would become even more so after [World War II]. . . .

The success of major league expansion and the dramatic rise in the values of sports franchises cannot be understood without reference to the impact of television. While franchising brought in important new revenues, the strategic objective for all professional sports from the 1960s onwards became to get, and increase the value of, national network television contracts. From the earliest days of sports television, it quickly became clear that television could augment sport's core audiences of already committed fans, both by taking "live" sport into new geographic regions and by presenting sports in ways designed to make them entertaining to new viewers. Replays and camera work helped television audiences to see things that stadium audiences often missed, while commentary sought to sustain excitement and to make viewers feel part of an important event. The latter was also true of radio, of course, but television's pictures were often worth a thousand words. In particular, television could bring athletes' faces into the living room, and this helped to "personalize" stars like Mickey Mantle, Joe Namath, and O.J. Simpson, adding to their celebrity status and hence the value of their images in endorsements. Televised sport was thus reworked according to the codes of the entertainment industry, and those who were successful at this (e.g., ABC's Monday Night NFL football telecasts, and in Canada CBC's "Hockey Night in Canada") built the biggest regular audiences in their respective countries.

This, not surprisingly, translated into lucrative advertising revenues, which in turn fueled spectacular increases in the monies the networks were willing to spend for exclusive rights to popular sports. The major sports would each develop their own methods of selling their product to television, with football, and later basketball, operating more collectively and sharing revenues more equally than either baseball or hockey—a difference that would produce important consequences that we shall return to shortly. In the 1960s, however, the most visible consequences of television money were increased profits, and players fighting for a share of these. With the successful establishment of player unions, all sports saw dramatic increases in player remuneration, culminating in the multi-million-dollar contracts that are commonplace today. This would have the effect of making owners dependent on steadily increasing the value of their television contracts and this, in turn, would influence the strategic objectives and geographic directions of future expansions.

National Audiences

All claimants to "major league" status need a strong presence in the major metropolitan markets, but they also need to position themselves in places seen as growing and affluent markets. Most importantly, in the 1960s, major leagues needed to be able to offer the networks the prospect of "national" audiences. This would mean that all of the established "major leagues" would expand into cities and regions where their sports were not historically major, and it would favor growing and underrepresented television markets—in California, Florida, Colorado, the Pacific northwest, and later the Carolinas—over cities, like Buffalo, whose television radius overlapped with the markets of established teams. It also led to the phenomenon of teams being promoted as state or regional representatives, even when (as in the case of the Denver Broncos or Portland Trailblazers) they still bore a civic name. Ultimately these dynamics (i.e., television and expansion) would promote interest in a variety of sports in cities and regions where one sport had traditionally dominated.

Here it is germane to return to the different ways that sports have sold themselves to (and through) television, and some of the consequences of these differences. It was arguably the NFL in the early 1960s that led the way in taking advantage of the opportunities afforded by network television. Under the leadership of commissioner Pete Rozelle, the league assumed control of the sale of televised football, and pioneered the idea of a single, nationally-televised game. Revenues from the first network contract (with CBS) in 1962 were divided equally among member teams, who were no longer able to telecast their own games locally. The model of a single national telecast would be extended in 1964 to the popular double header (a game in the east followed by one in the west), and later to Monday Night Football on ABC. However, the fact that all of these broadcasts were exclusive, and didn't have to compete with locally-televised games, built enormous and reliable *national* audiences, who in turn pulled in enormous dollars for the networks from national advertisers. . . .

This contrasts with the practice of baseball, which also sold the networks broadcast rights to a "Game of the Week," but the sport's commissioners could never secure the agreement of large market owners, in particular, to forego the sale of local television rights. This meant that national telecasts had to compete with a patchwork of locally and regionally televised games, and ratings suggested that local loyalties typically prevailed. Thus, although baseball attracted huge national audiences for the World Series, it has never succeeded in the way that football did in building them for regular season matches. The economic consequences are that the value of baseball advertising to the networks declined well below that of football, and the networks became resistant to paying the increases that owners now needed to fund their exploding payrolls. This, in turn, has sustained the importance of the revenues that owners get separately for local and regional rights. Yet this entrenches the economic divide between large market baseball teams (and, now, teams owned by superstations or regional sports networks), and their small market competitors. Through the late 1980s, the networks continued to pay significant sums for rights to major league baseball, because they wanted the World Series. However they increasingly didn't televise mid-season games that they had rights to, and the signs were clear that the constantly rising revenues of the past were over. The contract signed in 1993 marked an end to guaranteed revenues, and the beginning of a very different relationship between television and major league baseball.

The National Hockey League and National Basketball Association each have their own peculiar histories that differentiate them from the above "prototypes." The NHL has a long history as a national institution in Canada, and as noted above, CBC's hockey broadcasts have attracted Canada's first, and consistently largest, national audiences. However although the NHL had a short-lived contract with CBS in the early 1970s, it attracted abysmal American ratings and was not renewed. In this context, US teams have had to develop the revenue opportunities afforded by local and regional television. Some teams have done well by this, especially since the advent of regional sports networks (e.g., in New York, Boston). However the absence of a US network contract has had consequences not dissimilar to baseball, both economically (a growing divide between large and small market teams), and in the regional nature of audience interest. Even the Stanley Cup playoffs are not a national event in the United States.

The NBA, in contrast, has moved from a problem-plagued position in the late 1970s when only the playoffs attracted national interest, to a status in American popular culture that now rivals that of the NFL. Football's television revenues remain greater, but basketball's have risen dramatically to easily surpass those of baseball and hockey. From the time David Stern took over as commissioner, the league would follow the NFL model of centralizing control of broadcast rights and significantly reducing the competing product on the screen. The exclusive national exposure of the NFL's Sunday and Monday night broadcasts is harder to achieve in a sport that plays an eighty-two game season and schedules games throughout the week. However, the league has successfully imposed limits on local broadcasting (though not without opposition, notably from the Chicago Bulls), and the size and market value of the national audiences have risen sharply. There are other important factors in the NBA's remarkable ascendancy in the 1990s; and some of these, in particular merchandising and corporate marketing, will be addressed in the next section. . . .

Ultimately, the most far-reaching consequence of television and expansion in major league sports has been the gradual "delocalization" of sporting tastes and loyalties. At first, in the 1950s and 1960s, this simply meant the further popularization of major league sport, and a corresponding decline (that would later be partially reversed) in the fortunes of the minors. Through the 1970s and 1980s, "delocalization" would refer to the increasing incidence of franchise movements, and to the rupture of traditionally understood relationships between teams and cities that the phenomenon of the moveable franchise represents. Most generally, though, national television would encourage, and gradually normalize, the practice of fans identifying with teams based elsewhere, in contrast to older loyalties based in geography. Thus it was that the Dallas Cowboys became, for a time, "America's Team," while in later years national followings would develop for teams like the LA Raiders and Chicago Bulls. "Walk down any street in America and observe the diversity of team logos on caps, T-shirts, and bumper stickers. Fans for any team can turn up anywhere," and they register support of "their" teams not just by purchasing insignia clothing but by constituting large and geographically distributed television audiences. The significance of this tendency, which would become even more visible by the 1990s, is that it marks the gradual detachment of professional sports from loyalties and meanings based in place, and a normalization of the discourses of personal and consumer choice.

The New Economy of Pro Sports

We can illustrate this general proposition by examining some of the new "revenue streams" that have become important in professional sport: merchandising, corporate public relations, and cross-marketing. All of these trade on the symbolic meanings that can be attached to particular sports and sports celebrities, and their value rises as signifiers like the Chicago Bulls for example, or Wayne Gretzky, become meaningful to wider consumer audiences. Among the most visible symbolic commodities, of course, are the team caps and other merchandise that sport "official" major league logos. Baseball caps and hockey sweaters were historically a small revenue source for famous teams like the New York Yankees or Montreal Canadiens. However, the market for these items was tied to the team's historic prowess, and was typically confined to local boys for whom wearing a rival city's sweater was inconceivable. In the 1980s, the NFL and the NBA, in particular, showed that merchandise associated with nationally-followed teams—and individuals— could be promoted anywhere. They also showed that a coordinated approach to the promotion of licensed merchandise could make team gear fashionable in the adolescent and young adult "sportswear" markets. Insignia sportswear is, arguably, simply a variant on the promotion of wearable advertising, modelled so successfully by the makers of sport shoes (e.g., Nike, Adidas) and other casual wear (e.g., Gap, Tommy Hilfiger). However, it opened up enormous new potential revenues, as well as reinforcing the place of sports logos and colors in the symbolic language and landscape of North American youth culture. The irony is that it is now team colors and logos (and names), rather than a team's competitive prowess, that sell merchandise. This is demonstrated in the merchandising successes of expansion teams like the San Jose Sharks and Toronto Raptors, and it has normalized the selection of names and design of uniforms by marketing departments.

A related aspect of the economy of contemporary professional sports involves the marketing of stars. This is not a new phenomenon in show business, as we have observed, but it takes on new dimensions in the television era. Television has made sports stars more recognizable, and added to the overall presence of sport in contemporary popular culture. The National Basketball Association has taken particular advantage of television since the 1980s to associate the game with the skills and personalities of a series of stars: Magic Johnson and Larry Bird, Michael Jordan and Charles Barkley, Shaquille O'Neal and Grant Hill. Televised basketball's "visible heads" mean that viewers get vivid individual images, both of the extravagant skills of a Jordan, and the emotions and "attitude" out of which imaged personae have been constructed around men like Barkley and Rodman. The NBA has built on these advantages with spectacular success, as have the shoe companies Nike and Reebok. The effect has been to create an unprecedented series of black American celebrities, whose celebrity has in turn augmented the visibility of the league and the game in American (and now global) popular culture. . . .

It is important here to appreciate that the iconic status of a Jordan is not the result of skill alone, though skill is a necessary foundation. The construction of imaged celebrities is a promotional practice in itself and, when successful, it confers benefits on all partners in the exercise. Nike, in particular, attached its corporate persona to images of Michael Jordan, but when Jordan appeared in Nike advertisements in the early 1990s, he was adding to the global visibility of the Chicago Bulls, the NBA, and the game of basketball, as well as promoting Nike shoes. He was also, not incidentally, promoting himself and adding to his value as a promotional icon. Whether Nike and Jordan have helped to promote the NBA or vice versa is neither clear nor important. What this illustrates is that in "circuits of promotion" there are no obvious starting points and endpoints, but rather recursive and mutually reinforcing public texts that generate more visibility and more business for all concerned. It also illustrates that cultural commodities, including celebrities, can become vehicles for the promotion of more than one producer's product at once.

The most important developments in the sports business, however, follow from the rapid deployment of pay-tv technologies (i.e., cable and satellite services), and from technological and corporate developments that point towards tighter vertical integration in the communications and "infotainment" industries. Subscription television achieved near complete market penetration across the US and Canada by the early 1980s, not least because there was widespread consumer interest in the multiplicity of specialty channels that the new technologies could offer. Yet it was access to sports and movies that attracted the keenest interest and appeared decisive in persuading customers to subscribe to cable or to choose one service provider over another. In addition, specialty sports channels attracted the male audiences that many advertisers wanted to target, and they did so more cost-effectively than the national networks. In this context, regional sports channels carrying the games of local teams provided more visibility for sports on television, and they provided an important revenue stream for the teams whose games they carried. However, in baseball and hockey where there was less central (i.e., league) control over broadcast rights, this would further sharpen the revenue gap between larger and small market teams, while also weakening the value of national network contracts. . . .

Sports and Branded Products

All of these developments, it can be suggested, represent a new stage in the commodification of sport, and point to the further incorporation of mediated sport, in particular, into a postmodern "economy of signs." In this economy, the market value of televised sport is increased exponentially by communications technologies that multiply distributive capacity while allowing distributors to charge. In this economy, the construction of symbolic meanings is crucial to adding value to many kinds of branded products, whether these are experiential products like NBA basketball or the Olympics, or material products like sneakers and sweaters and colas. In either case, it is the product name and the symbolic associations it carries that attract new consumers, and establish its value as a commodity-sign. . . . In this economy, finally, where images and logos can be readily transmitted across thousands of miles and across cultural borders, the ultimate audience is global, combining the affluent markets of Europe and North America and mining the huge potential of the "emerging" markets of Latin America and Asia. "In Planet Reebok," as their advertising puts it, "there are no boundaries."

Thus in sport, even though the initial efforts of the National Football League to expand into Europe in the late 1980s met with only limited success, as have efforts to establish professional soccer in America, it is clear in the late 1990s that most of the major professional sports and the television conglomerates that now have investments in them are exploring how to reach global audiences. All the major professional sports seek to demonstrate to transnational advertisers that they can attract global audiences—in the manner of the Olympics. For those that succeed in demonstrating their marketing potential in what are now global circuits of promotion, the stakes are almost unlimited, in terms of merchandising and television revenues and the allied promotional revenues outlined above.

Pro Sports as Show Business

John R. Gerdy

John R. Gerdy is visiting professor of sports administration at Ohio University and the author of *Sports: The All-American Addiction*, from which this article is excerpted. In it, he protests what he feels are the negative effects of the confluence of sports and entertainment in popular culture. In his opinion, the games themselves have become secondary to their entertainment value and the profit that they can generate. Gerdy contends that "sportainment" is negatively influencing American culture, not merely reflecting values of a capitalist, media-driven society.

THERE WAS A TIME WHEN THE THOUGHT OF comparing professional wrestling and the NFL, NBA, or major college sporting events was unthinkable. The lines of distinction were simply too clear. Wrestling was staged. Rivalries were created and then hyped. What transpired outside of the ring was every bit a part of the show as what went on in it. It was entertainment, pure and simple. *Real* sports were something entirely different. They were serious. It was the game that mattered. But there is very little difference between today's professional, and increasingly, college sporting events and an Extreme Championship Wrestling (ECW) or World Wrestling Federation (WWF) event. In fact, the NBA has gotten so far away from being about sport, that the league does not feel the game is interesting enough to entertain fans without help of an organist or taped snippets of deafening "rev up

■

the fan" music blaring incessantly in the background . . . during play! Even the ECW respects their "sport" enough to turn the music off during the match.

To describe an NBA or NFL game or the Final Four as a "sporting event" is no longer accurate. These events are entertainment extravaganzas, subject to all the promotional and marketing gimmicks of a three ring circus. Even the issue of games being predetermined can be called into question. Concerns regarding game fixing at the college level are increasing. And there is always "league interest" in certain teams advancing into the next round of the playoffs. Do you think NBA and NBC executives breathed a sigh of relief when Michael Jordan and the Chicago Bulls finally put away the Indiana Pacers to move on to the 1998 Finals? Indiana versus Utah? What kind of television ratings would that generate?

Today, sport is packaged, merchandised, and marketed as entertainment. It is more about money, television ratings, advertising rates, and corporate sky boxes than it is about sport. Think it's simply a coincidence that ESPN is the abbreviation for the Entertainment Sports Programming Network? As Dick Vitale might say, "It's showbiz, Baby!"

Our "Sportainment" Culture

In his book entitled *Spoiled Sport*, John Underwood writes about sport's better days. While he does not claim that sport of yesteryear was "cleaner" (there has always been enough cheating, bad sportsmanship, arrogant and immature athletes, unscrupulous agents, and greedy owners to go around), he does, however, maintain that sport was "purer" because it had far less commercial value to be manipulated for economic gain. Thus, Underwood contends, it was simpler and more appealing. Because of its growing public appeal, it is increasingly being manipulated by "marketplace ethics" in the quest for greater economic return for investors, owners, and television networks—from the flow of the game being interrupted for television timeouts, to the blaring music played during the game, to labor strife and lockouts, to the smoke, fireworks, and glittering lights of longer and longer player introductions. In Underwood's words, "It has been transformed into economic snake oil. From something wonderful, it has been made grotesque by commerce. It has been distorted and polluted by money, and the never-ending quest for more. It has been appropriated by a growing army of owner-entrepreneurs who made a remarkable discovery after the 1950's: that sport was not sport at all but a tool for extracting incredible riches from the sports-hungry populace."

Sport has become a commodity, to be bought, sold, and used to generate profit. And, as is natural with any commodity, it eventually becomes "corporatized." In the movie *Rollerball*, James Cahn plays Jonathan, the world's best rollerball player, a sport that is remindful of the roller derby days of Joanie Weston and the San Francisco Bay Area Bombers. But this game has a far more deadly twist. Competitors fight for possession of a cantaloupe-sized solid-steel ball. Points are scored when the ball is deposited in a small goal. Heavily plated motorcycles circle the track alongside players on skates, who are outfitted in weaponry that include leather arm and hand gear adorned with blunt metal spikes and plating. Competitors are routinely dragged off the playing surface with what are depicted as life-threatening or life-ending injuries. Meanwhile, play does not stop.

Interestingly, Jonathan does not play for a city, state, or country but rather a company, a multinational corporation, competing against other worldwide corporate giants. While it is easy to dismiss *Rollerball* as merely an entertaining, futuristic, sci-fi musing, the fact is, we may not be that far from the "corporate sport" depicted in this movie. Just who is it that members of the Los Angeles Dodgers play for anyway? The people of L.A. or the Fox Corporation that owns the team? Does Tom Glavine pitch for the city of Atlanta or the Time-Warner Corporation? And what corporate conglomerate owns the New York Knicks and the Rangers these days? Increasingly, it is more likely that "your city's" team is not "your city's" at all, but rather, a corporation's—representing simply one commodity in its vast multinational asset portfolio. And with B Sky B, Rupert Murdoch's British Satellite TV company, purchasing Manchester United, Britain's richest soccer club for $1 billion, the days of the family-owned professional franchise are numbered.

Rollerball's "championship" game, a game where there were no rules and no time limit, where the "contest" ended when all competitors but one was left alive, presented a telling glimpse of our sports future. With the blood sport Extreme Fighting gaining popularity, a "sport" where the contestants are locked in a cage and the only rule is "no eye gouging," *Rollerball's* "end game" does not seem so far-fetched.

The result of the "corporatization" of sport, is that, as in any business, all decisions are influenced by the bottom line. According to Underwood,

> The padrones of sport are milking it dry. They have inflated ticket prices to the point where a trip to the ballpark for the average family is now an adventure in high finance. They move their clubs and players from city to city like gypsies, or threaten to if demands for a new stadium or a better lease or a few million dollars' worth of improvements are not met. They cater to the whims of television by playing games at all hours and twisting the seasons around and stretching them out so that they overlap and smother each other in the endless grubbing for money.

The line between sport and entertainment has become hopelessly blurred. In fact, they have become one. Increasingly, in this sports/entertainment hybrid, it is the television network executives who are calling the shots, packaging, promoting, and now, even creating, sports entertainment events. The Goodwill Games, for example, were created and run by the Turner Network, now owned by Time-Warner. To attract more Generation X viewers for corporate sponsors, ESPN invented the X-Games. These "games" were created, not necessarily as sporting events, but rather as television entertainment programming—soap operas with sweat. Briefly, we even had the Extreme Football League (XFL), a joint venture between Vince McMahon, owner of the World Wrestling Federation, and NBC Sports, where players were encouraged to smash quarterbacks and to date the cheerleaders. Sport purists have raised the obvious questions about the effect of such preprogrammed "sportainment" on the integrity and purity of athletic competition. They are wasting their breath. There are no issues of integrity, purity, and sanctity of such "competition" because they aren't sporting events at all. They are entertainment spectacles. This evolution, however, has come at a cost.

[According to Elliot J. Gorn and Warren Goldstein, authors of *A Brief History of American Sports*:]

> Sports have become valuable entertainment goods, and new mass media, particularly radio and television, have at once sold and shaped those goods. The financial opportunities opened up by the marketing of sports have enticed the most talented people onto our playing fields, have encouraged new ways to develop that talent, and have given us ever-improving, often astonishing displays of physical excellence. . . . Even as our athletes soar to unheard-of heights, we are in danger of losing sight of all values beyond winning. In the worst case, we become complicit in a system that makes money its god; we find ourselves watching televised spectacles that bury athletic competition with commentator's babble, with advertisers' useless products, with a cult of fame and glamour; and we ignore the destruction of our most physically gifted young people's bodies through drugs pushed by a systemic compulsion to win at all costs.

But we have moved beyond simply winning at any cost. Today, the driving force behind sports is profit. And in sports, profits result not necessarily from winning, but from being entertaining. But in transforming our athletes into entertainers, we have trivialized sport. Those things that we have long valued in sport—its ability to promote good health, develop character, encourage sportsmanship, and bring people together—are simply no longer important. It is the athlete's or team's ability to drive television ratings and profit margins that is of paramount importance in our sportainment culture. It is a sad day when Latrell Sprewell's entertainment value actually increases as a result of choking his coach. From an entertainment value standpoint, Sprewell is worth more money because more people are going to tune in to see if he flips out again. In our sportainment society, athletes' deeds and examples in areas such as sportsmanship and character are relegated to the back seat because it is their entertainment value and potential to generate profits that drive their value to the team, the league, and the television networks. Sadly, the game itself has become secondary to its entertainment value, as are the players and fans who support it. . . .

An ESPN Mentality

Television has affected virtually every aspect of our games, distorting not only when but also how they are played. [As Gorn and Goldstein write:] "Because television networks make money by, in effect, renting audiences to advertisers, they have considerably less interest in the internal structures, particular histories and traditions, or distinctive rhythms of a given sport—except insofar as they affect the number of viewers." The most obvious example of this negative influence is how television timeouts lengthen games and disrupt their natural rhythm. Starting times for World Series games require that children on the East Coast stay up past midnight to see the last out and college basketball games are scheduled to meet the programming needs of television executives rather than the academic needs of the "student-athletes" who play them.

We have been tricked into believing that the only worthwhile sport is "big-time sport." And, to be considered big-time sport, it must be on television. "The real impact of television lies in its pervasiveness: that there are so few sporting experiences that have not at least been exposed to—and therefore in an important sense measured by—the professional ethos of televised sports" [explain Gorn and Goldstein]. We have been duped into believing that unless you are worthy of an ESPN highlight, you are not worthy as an athlete. It is no longer enough to play simply for the camaraderie, the intrinsic values gained, or the sheer joy of participation.

The impact of this ESPN mentality on the individual athlete is tremendous as it is the driving force behind how an athlete determines his or her "success." Most athletes are conditioned to believe that the only successful athletic career is one which ends in the Olympics, NBA, NFL, or other major professional leagues. I witnessed the tragic results of this throughout my athletic career, particularly while playing professionally in the Continental Basketball Association. Despite having athletic careers that provided the chance to get a college education, travel the world, and open countless doors of opportunity, many of us considered ourselves failures because we didn't play in the NBA. Many never recover from having been a "failure" at the ripe old age of twenty-two.

The Lure of the "Big Time"

Our obsession with wanting to be a part of "big-time sport" is so pervasive that we will do most anything to be connected to it, no matter how distantly. Sports apparel advertisements implore us to "look like the pros." Sports equipment manufacturers tell us that their products will help us to "play like the pros." We wear our T-shirts, hats, and parkas adorned with our favorite team logos like a badge of honor. Family, friends, coaches, teachers, and other assorted "wannabes" and hangers-on "invest" in the careers of potential future star athletes, providing favors and clamoring for their attention and affection like a toddler reaching out for his mother. And when the athlete "fails," it is often these wannabes who somehow feel betrayed. The athlete feels that he has let these people down, regardless of whether he ever wanted them along for the ride. It is a burden that many athletes find stifling. And it is a sad commentary on our lives when we invest so much time, energy, and emotion chasing another's elusive dream of athletic stardom. . . .

The big-time sport mentality's effect is so pervasive it can overtake an entire city, region, or state. Municipal leaders actually believe that the only way they can ever be considered a big-time city is if they house one of the major sports league's teams. Time and time again, precious tax dollars are appropriated to subsidize extraordinarily wealthy team owners and their millionaire players. Despite the fact that fans may have to drive over pot-holed roads to get to them, new stadiums and arenas are built on land donated by the city, complete with luxury suites, prime office space, and state-of-the-art practice facilities, all financed by taxpayers. And as thanks, we get the privilege of getting to buy a Coke in a souvenir plastic cup for seven dollars. . . .

This is where we are. This is what sport in America has become. It is no longer about the participants or about playing for the sheer joy of competing. It is not about health, education, social mobility, or racial equality. It is about entertainment, money, ego, image, and getting on television. It is not even about getting our fifteen minutes of fame, but rather latching on to someone else's fifteen minutes by wearing logo-laden sportswear and cheering loudly. In sum, we have lost perspective.

Apologists are likely to dismiss these criticisms, claiming that sport is merely a reflection of the values and behaviors of our society. Perhaps they are correct. Perhaps the evolution of sport in America is simply reflective of our societal values—capitalistic, media driven, and consumption based. Certainly there is an element of truth to such a claim. It is, however, too simplistic an argument, a cop-out to explain the unacceptable behavior of athletes and the warped values that drive sports teams and institutions. While there may have been a time when the values and behaviors associated with organized athletics merely reflected those of society, that is no longer the case. Organized sport in America has become too pervasive an influence to be considered merely a reflection of cultural values. You cannot have it both ways. You cannot claim that athletics develops character, builds community, and promotes positive values but, when the dark side of organized athletics rears its ugly head, claim that sports is merely a reflection of society. The relationship between the values of sport and the values of our culture is symbiotic. While cultural values certainly influence what we see and hear about on the fields of play, the inverse is also true. What occurs on the fields of play influences cultural values and norms.

Not What It Is Supposed to Be

The culture of organized sport in America has changed so dramatically that we can hardly recognize it as sport anymore. Nicholas Dawidoff, author of *The Catcher Was a Spy: The Mysterious Life of Moe Berg*, aptly described the shifting culture of American sports in a *New York Times* op-ed piece regarding Major League baseball's decision to open its 2000 season in Japan with two games between the New York Mets and the Chicago Cubs. "When the corporate instincts that have given us chain stores, fast-food restaurants, and theme parks invade our pastimes, they bleed them of the dash of strangeness that attracted us in the first place. If you market your culture too much, marketing becomes your culture."

This dramatic change has presented us with a troubling dilemma. Although we may continue to watch and support sport, perhaps more out of habit than anything else, we don't particularly like what it represents, what it has become, and how it makes us act. The problem is that we don't know what to do about it. So, like a drug addict we continue to inject it into our minds and bodies. It is as if we have ordered filet mignon from the menu only to be served sirloin steak. Do you simply eat the sirloin because you are hungry and it is not worth the time and effort to return it? After all, it is still red meat. Or, do we return it and demand what we have paid for?

Of course, organized sport in America is not all bad. There are plenty of coaches and athletic programs committed to instilling positive values in participants. There are thousands of athletes who benefit greatly from athletic participation. And there is a degree of value in sports' entertainment function. But while it is not all bad, it is clearly not what it is supposed to be. The fact is, an honest, rational argument can be made that organized sports' overall influence within our culture has become more negative than positive, that the moral basis upon which it was built has crumbled to dust and, as a result, has left it devoid of meaning. Merely the fact that such an argument can be made should certainly give us reason to pause.

Public vs. Corporate Interests in the Pro Sports Industry

John Solomon

Journalist John Solomon writes frequently on sports and politics. In the following selection, he criticizes the manner in which pro sports leagues treat their fans, citing taxpayer-subsidized stadiums and the high cost of attending games. He blames the excesses of pro sports on the sports media, who are hesitant to cover pro sports' failings; lawmakers, who are heavily influenced by the pro sports lobby; and the fans themselves, who continue to support their favorite teams despite the rising expense of doing so. Solomon proposes a number of reforms that should be made, including reducing and regulating public subsidies for sports teams and investigating possible monopolistic behavior by media conglomerates and pro sports leagues.

WHEN JOHN CROTTY AND PETER LYONS LEARNED the National Football League's New York Jets were being put up for sale this summer [1999], they asked each other a seemingly naive question: why can't Jets fans like us buy the team ourselves?

The 30-year-old boyhood friends from New York decided to find out. They created a website, BuyTheJets.com, and

■

John Solomon, "Whose Game Is It, Anyway?" *Washington Monthly*, vol. 31, December 1999, p. 31. Copyright © 1999 by Washington Monthly Publishing, LLC. Reproduced by permission.

launched a bid. "Upon receiving significant expressions from you, the fans, we will assemble an ownership vehicle," they wrote in their site manifesto, which included a guarantee that the team would never leave the New York area. In just two months, 11,000 people signed up and made tentative financial commitments totaling more than $20 million.

Despite the overwhelming response, however, the NFL would not even send BuyTheJets a prospectus. The league prohibits public ownership, with the one grandfathered exception of the Green Bay Packers.

Nevertheless, the idea clearly touched a nerve with a public wanting both to dream about owning a team and to send a message that fans deserve a greater voice in pro sports. The NFL's decision to summarily disregard the BuyTheJets bid was fittingly emblematic of the unsportsmanlike conduct with which the industry too often treats its passionate and loyal supporters.

In addition to recurring work stoppages, ticket prices have risen more than three times the rate of inflation over the last decade. A major league baseball seat cost 10% more on average this past [1999] season than it did the year before. Including the $2 sodas and $3 hot dogs, it runs a family of four $267 to attend an NBA game, up 31 percent from just four years ago, according to the Team Marketing Report.

Worse, taxpayers are routinely forced to ante up even more dough to satisfy "if you don't build it, I will leave" owner demands for new facilities. In 1999 and 2000, pro teams will be playing in new homes costing the public $9 billion. In Seattle, the Mariners' mediocre record playing in new Safeco Field pales in comparison to its performance paying for it. After a stadium ballot measure was rejected, the Mariners made a deal with the state legislature that they would pick up only $45 million of the $417 million price tag on the facility but would also pay for overruns. Safeco went $100 million over budget, and now the Mariners are refusing to pay. The team, principally owned by Nintendo of America, says it needs the public to cover the extra cost in order for it to compete financially.

Owners complain about the financial hardship involved in running pro teams. Yet, peer behind the doom and gloom talk, and it becomes clear that teams have never been more valuable. Franchise prices—both existing and expansion—continue to go up. The NFL awarded its newest expansion team to Houston [in fall 1999] for $700 million, up from the $140 million entry price of just five years ago. In November 1999, the Cleveland Indians were sold for a record $320 million by Richard Jacobs who bought the team in 1986 for $45 million. As Yogi Berra might say, buying a sports team is such a bad deal, everyone wants one.

The pro sports business does provide Americans with a unique, wildly popular and state-of-the-art product. That's why Crotty and Lyons have been able to sign up thousands of people, and why there's a line of billionaires ahead of them. That success, however, doesn't mean it should be able to play without any refereeing.

The $10 billion industry is run by almost completely unregulated monopolies. Elected officials seem to confuse governmental oversight with the view from their front row seats. In addition, pro sports' failings don't get the coverage they deserve in the press. The national sports media are frequently "league partners" or even franchise owners (Fox and Time Warner are good examples), rendering their journalism on the subject less than objective. The local press does a good job covering the games but doesn't follow the larger off-the-field issues as thoroughly. And sports talk radio for the most part prefers to stir up public discontent rather than harness it constructively In short, no one is playing defense for the public.

Twenty years ago, Ralph Nader tried to form a sports consumer group to organize fan interest. He failed, but now he's trying again. "It's a strange thing. It isn't anything like the car, food or drug industries. People can be angry and pay through the nose, but they'll still root for their team," he says. Nader is a perfect example—a boyhood New York Yankees fan who (believe it or not) has continued to root for the Bronx Bombers, albeit a little less rabidly, through the reign of George Steinbrenner.

Nader's effort faces huge challenges. Organizing fans—with their parochial and often opposing interests—is about as easy as trying to get fans to agree on who's better, [Sammy] Sosa or [Mark] McGwire. Perspectives on revenue sharing and franchise relocation differ from one ballpark to the next. Growing cities desperate to have a team of their own want to make franchise movement easier; cities eager to hang on to prestige organizations obviously don't.

Additionally, fans have never been willing to use their ultimate leverage over owners and players: their butts. Despite the public vitriol over the NBA lockout, hoop enthusiasm returned to their arena seats and TV rooms when play resumed. It is an interesting paradox: the public has never been so angry, but pro sports have never been so popular. For most fans, sports are an escape from real life; they're not going to punish themselves to punish the industry.

Unfortunately, teams don't always have the same loyalty to their fans. Sports franchises in the 1990s threaten and sometimes even leave communities that have been devoted to them for generations. Even worse, teams use this devotion to force local governments into lucrative subsidies for the development of new stadiums. Earlier in the century, most pro sports stadiums were entirely privately financed. In the '60s and '70s, a number of cities built dual-purpose facilities which they would then rent to baseball and football franchises. The cities themselves kept much of the revenue from concessions, parking and stadium advertising. In the '90s, that almost seems quaint.

Despite simmering concern that pro sports are taking advantage of the American public, the sports industry has managed to keep legislators away. The promise (or threat) of new (or lost) franchises adds juice to the industry's lobbying efforts. And it doesn't hurt that so many legislators are sports junkies. Major league baseball provided tickets to more than 200 legislators, staffers and their families to [1998's] World Series at sold-out Yankee Stadium. You can bet that there will also be a healthy Washington presence in Atlanta for [2000's] Super Bowl whether the Redskins are in it or not.

The industry's high-powered lobby has long been augmented by the connections and financial contributions of its owners. In the last election cycle, according to the Center for Responsive Politics, Jerry Reinsdorf of the Chicago White Sox and Chicago Bulls made contributions totaling $51,250; Micky Arison of the Miami Heat donated $60,500; and Abe Pollin of the Washington Wizards and the MCI Center gave $85,000.

Representative of the strength of the pro sports business in general and Pollin in particular are the recent changes in the congressional gift ban regulations. Thanks in part to Pollin's lobbying, House members are now allowed to receive gifts up to a value of $50. As any sports fan could tell you, $50 is not going to buy you a luxury box seat to an NBA game. That is unless you're a congressman or senator at the MCI Center where club seats for Washington Capitals and Wizards games have been priced at . . . $48. It may be the only ticket in sports whose price will not outpace inflation.

Over on the other side of the Hill, the Senate Ethics Committee made an equally dubious ruling on luxury box pricing. The committee decided the valuation, for the purpose of the gift ban, would be "the price of the seat in closest proximity bearing a face value." As luxury boxes (a.k.a. Sky Boxes) are often at the top of the building, the Senate is valuing them at the rate of the cheap "nosebleed" seats. Of course, nosebleed seats don't have plush couches or televisions.

Congressmen are also known to get a little weak in the knees at the star power that sports lobbyists can summon when it suits their purposes. "I know it sounds a little crazy," observes a Senate aide who has worked on sports-related issues, "but an autograph from Cal Ripken, and then a 'thank you' note from Roger Clemens can have a lot of impact."

Given the emotional nature of pro sports and the big money involved, the best mechanism for addressing this complex situation would be a special commission convened by either congress or the president to undertake the first-ever comprehensive review of sports policy. The commission would comprise knowledgeable stakeholders—league management, owners, players' unions, media, political leaders and fans—who would take a careful look at sports policy issues, including franchise movement, stadium construction, antitrust, ticket prices and community ownership. Sports policy is rarely discussed in a careful, in-depth way, but instead usually under the gun in an overheated atmosphere after a team has threatened to leave. Why would the industry participate? Perhaps to avert the possibility that local legislatures will take matters into their own hands, or that a spurned town or city will launch a lawsuit that will imperil the delicate legal balance that the leagues have created. A national commission could also be a vehicle for the NFL, NBA and NHL to argue for an expansion of their antitrust powers.

There are a number of ideas that a commission should consider:

• First, the sports industry needs to be weaned off the public construction subsidies it receives. Senator Arlen Specter has proposed a bill that would require the pro sports leagues to set aside 10 percent of their television revenues for a special stadium construction fund. Under Specter's proposal, if the leagues do not create the stadium fund, they will lose the broadcasting antitrust exemption granted to them by congress in 1962. That exemption allows the teams to pool their media rights for sale. On the other hand, if the teams agree to the stadium fund, all of the pro sports leagues will be granted an exemption from federal regulation along the lines currently enjoyed by major league baseball—which continues to benefit from a 1922 Supreme Court ruling that the national pastime cannot be regulated by the federal government because it is not interstate commerce. This may actually be good for fans. If a league is exempt from federal regulation, then its commissioner can guide the movement of franchises with less concern about being sued under federal antitrust law. Pro baseball has not had a team move since 1972.

But television money may not be the right lever, given that contracts vary widely by sport. The NFL has established a special construction allowance for its teams, but much more of a private contribution is necessary. One shining model of this from another sport is San Francisco Giants' owner Peter Magowan, who raised $319 million almost entirely through private sources for Pacific Bell Park, which opens [in 2000]. Magowan sold $130 million in commercial sponsorships and then leveraged those commitments into $170 million in loans. PacBell Park is one of only three major pro facilities built in this decade entirely with private funds. Granted, this approach may not be feasible or suitable in all markets, but Magowan deserves enormous credit for accomplishing what more owners should be attempting.

• The federal government needs to examine what it can do to reduce the spiraling corporate welfare bidding war between different communities over teams. No city or state likes being at the beck and call of sports owners. But, like a presidential candidate in favor of campaign finance reform, it is difficult to stop the competition unilaterally. Legislation authored by Senator Daniel P. Moynihan and Representative Barney Frank would eliminate a federal tax exemption that currently applies to financing for the construction of new sports facilities. This makes sense. Research has largely discredited the idea that stadiums are engines of economic development. Why, then, should federal taxpayers be helping cities pay for them? Existing law is a textbook example of concentrated benefits and distributive costs, and the Moynihan/Frank bill is one of the rare economic initiatives enthusiastically backed by both *The Wall Street Journal* and *The Nation*.

A more ambitious proposal, offered by Representative David Minge, would slap a federal excise tax on economic incentives that states and localities use to recruit and hold on to companies. The idea would discourage the bidding wars that erupt when cities fight over pro sports teams. Rep. Minge's proposal to tax state and local economic development incentives goes more directly and comprehensively at the problem. But it would have significant ramifications beyond sports, and therefore is only a starting point for discussion.

• Congress should reconsider the automatic 50 percent write off corporations receive on sports tickets. New arenas are built with the confidence that businesses will purchase—and deduct—expensive luxury seating. This has the perverse result that average citizens end up paying for the tax break that raises the prices of sporting events out of their reach.

• When a major public investment is made in stadiums and arenas, it should be subject to approval by referendum. Though the result doesn't necessarily dictate ultimate government policy, the process at least makes for a more open discussion of the issue. And, it was a referendum defeat that led Peter Magowan to try to finance the PacBell Park privately.

• If the public is going to contribute to stadium construction, local governments should be getting something tangible—i.e., low price ticket set aside, a revenue royalty, or a stay-put guarantee. Beginning [in 1999], the NBA has mandated that each team make 500 seats available before every game at $10/ticket. [In November 1999], President Clinton visited Newark to highlight the owners of the New Jersey Nets who are donating team profits to local youth development groups. With top league officials in attendance, Clinton implored pro owners to: "Think about the obligations owed to the people in your city. Make investment in your community second only to your priorities to bring home the championship trophy." But the role of sports teams in communities cannot be separated from construction financing, franchise movement and ticket prices. In addition, if President Clinton believes community-oriented ownership is the ideal, why doesn't he support allowing the public to bid for their teams along the lines of BuyTheJets.com? Rep. Earl Blumenauer's "Give Fans A Chance Act" would require leagues to allow community ownership, which is currently either explicitly prohibited or discouraged. Blumenauer isn't saying every team should be publicly owned, only that other ownership models should be considered.

• Government regulators also need to keep a closer eye on sports television, particularly as media companies like Fox, Time Warner, and Cablevision are increasingly doubling as team owners. If, for example, Cablevision purchases the New York Jets or Mets as has been rumored, the company would control three teams, two television networks and a cable system in the New York area. That content and distribution control is somewhat reminiscent of the type of vertical integration outlawed in the film business earlier in the century, which resulted in movie studios having to sell their theaters.

When it comes to looking after the interests of the public, it's not just politicians who have dropped the ball. Despite the proliferation of channels and programming, television isn't covering sports policy or consumer issues effectively. It's possible that the relationship with the sports industry is just too symbiotic. Typical is ESPN's current advertising campaign for "SportsCenter" (its nightly news program), which features pro athletes singing the praises of the show and its announcers. (It also may be that journalists have a different experience from their viewers and readers; they don't, for example, pay for tickets, refreshments and parking.) The print media has done a better job than television, but it still falls far short. Though many newspapers now have a sports media reporter, few cover the sports business, law, and political beats with any regularity.

Sports talk radio, which has grown meteorically to 250 stations nationwide, would appear to be well suited for the role of consumer advocate. But too many hosts either provoke listeners irresponsibly, aren't willing to be critical at all, or don't have enough knowledge to have an impact.

A strong and responsible national fans consumer group could also have a positive role. If Ralph Nader can't get his organization going, maybe Frank Stadulis will have more luck with his nascent USFANS. The former IBM executive is pursuing the same goal of organizing public discontent with a different approach. He's trying to create a mini-Internet sports portal and even hopes to give fans a chance to play in the online equivalent of the Super Bowl, an IPO. It's not your typical consumer advocacy model. But it's not inconceivable that a dot com might be more appropriate than a dot org in an industry whose mantra is "show me the money."

Professional sports deliver a uniquely successful product, and they should not be recklessly tampered with. But that very success—and the concomitant emotional connection of the public—underscores why addressing these issues is so important. However, there is not one magic solution to bring more balance, accountability, and fiscal sanity back to how the government deals with professional sports. One home run swing won't win the game, which is why a special sports commission would be the right first step.

"A lot of people depend on us for their daily feelings," observed George Steinbrenner in the midst of the Yankees' World Series celebration. "Our job is to make them happy."

The professional sports industry does exactly that on the field. But it still has a lot of work to do off of it. It's time that the fans, whose dollars have fueled the growth and made everyone else rich, have some say in how sports are governed.

BuyTheJets' Peter Lyons and John Crotty tried to do just that. Even though their bid was not considered, they feel they have helped raised the issue of public representation in pro sports. [Robert Wood Johnson IV bought the Jets in early 2000.] Despite his bad experience, Lyons, like a typical fan, says he has not soured on the sport nor on his team. "I love pro football and I love the Jets," he says with a laugh. "I'll always be a Jets fan even if I can't be a Jets owner."

CHAPTER

5

America's Obsession with Sports and Sports Stars

Fans and Fanatics

Douglas T. Putnam

Douglas T. Putnam is an attorney and the author of
Controversies of the Sports World, from which the following selection is excerpted. In it, he discusses the
intense passion that many sports fans have for their
favorite teams and sports. These "sportsaholics" indulge their obsession by tuning in to the widespread
media coverage of sports, collecting the seemingly
limitless amount of team-licensed merchandise that is
available, and by participating in "fantasy" leagues.
Some fans have also carried their obsession too far,
writes Putnam, stalking athletes or becoming violent
when their team loses.

AS A GRADUATE STUDENT IN SPORTS PSYCHOL-
ogy at the University of Florida, Charles Hillman knew that
the school's football fans were passionately devoted to the
Florida Gators, the 1996 national champions and a perennial
power in the Southeastern Conference. He did not know how
strong their devotion was until he conducted an experiment
that reached an interesting conclusion. For the most rabid
Florida Gator fans, watching their team perform on the football field each Saturday is better than having sex.

Hillman recruited fifty volunteers and classified them according to their interest level—low, moderate, or high—in
Florida Gator football. Then he used scientific instruments to
measure their heart rate and brain activity while they viewed a
series of images. The series included images of violence, neu-
tral objects such as tables and chairs, scenes of Florida football
games, and pictures of couples entwined in amorous embraces.

All three groups of volunteers measured similar reactions,

■

except when the football scenes were displayed. At those moments the most fervent Gator fans had reactions that measured very near the top of the two scales that Hillman had devised—one ranging from very unpleasant to very pleasant, the other from calm to excited. To determine how absorbed the volunteers were in the images, Hillman also used a sudden, sharp noise called a startle probe. As they viewed the lovemaking couples, the high-level Gator fans heard the startle probe loud and clear. But as they watched pictures of their beloved team in action, they became so deeply absorbed that they were much less aware of it. As one professor explained, "There were fewer brain resources available" when the fans were being treated to scenes of their favorite gridiron heroes.

To anyone who knows or lives with a passionate sports fan, the amusing conclusion reached by Hillman's study does not seem unusual. There are few, if any, other activities in modern America that excite as many people to as great an extent as watching sports events. It makes little difference if the sport being viewed is auto racing, baseball, basketball, football, or ice hockey. Each of those sports has a large and zealous following. For a sizable percentage of the fans, watching sports is the central focus of their lives.

Vicki Tucky of Clintonville, Ohio, knows how strong the passion for sports can be. Her husband David, a Cleveland native, enrolled at Ohio State University because of its successful football teams. He proposed to her with a message on the scoreboard at Cleveland Stadium before a National Football League (NFL) game between the Browns and the Cincinnati Bengals. He planned the conception of their son in 1996 so that the birth would not conflict with the major league baseball (MLB) playoffs, when he would be focused on the fortunes of the Cleveland Indians. Unlike many other spouses, Vicki Tucky accepts her husband's love of sports. She even admits to a love for the Cincinnati Bengals herself. "I put sports above most aspects of my life and I'm not ashamed of it," says David. "As long as I'm not hurting anybody, I plan to keep on doing it."

Millions of Fanatics

Millions of other people plan to keep doing it too. And although a huge majority of today's most intense sports fans are male, interest among women has grown in recent years. The NFL claims that its fan base is 44 percent female, up from 33 percent in 1990. That translates into 40 million fans, 400,000 of whom enter stadiums each week to watch the games in person. "Women are of critical importance to us," says Sara Levinson, the president of NFL Properties, the league's merchandising division. "They control the TV dial on Sunday afternoons and decide what sports their kids will get involved in. We have to make these gatekeepers comfortable."

Men and women alike can count on plenty of help from the new services and technological innovations that have been developed to meet the desires of hard-core fans. The Entertainment Sports Programming Network (ESPN) began broadcasting in 1979 with the goal of providing sports coverage twenty-four hours per day, seven days per week. It now reaches more than 70 million households in the United States, about 70 percent of all homes with television. Viewers also can watch ESPN2, a second network that began broadcasting in 1994, and the Golf Channel, devoted entirely to a sport with the loyal following that advertisers crave. Digital satellite systems such as Primestar and DIRECTV allow fans to view events on hundreds of cable television channels. For a subscription fee paid each season, pro football fans can purchase NFL Sunday Ticket, which provides access to all of the games played each Sunday instead of only the ones telecast in particular viewing areas. Pro basketball fans can enjoy similar viewing options with NBA League Pass. DIRECTV also offers NHL Center Ice for hockey, MLB Extra Innings for baseball, and MLS/ESPN Shootout for soccer. On radio, there are now more than 150 stations that feature sports talk, around-the-clock discussions among the host and the listening audience of all aspects of the sports world.

Fans need not be satisfied with watching games on television or listening to sports talk on radio. There are many other outlets for their passion. Fantasy baseball camps give them a chance to test their skills on the diamond against big league stars of the past. For a die-hard Boston Red Sox fan, there may be no greater thrill than standing in the batter's box trying to hit a knuckleball thrown by former Sox hurler Luis Tiant. Fantasy Leagues allow baseball, football, basketball, and hockey devotees with a bent for statistics and strategy to create their own teams and compete against other league members. Sports Tours, Inc., a Massachusetts-based travel agency, offers vacation junkets to "couch potatoes" who spend most of their time in front of the television watching their favorite teams. Among the most popular destinations are the Baseball Hall of Fame in Cooperstown, New York, and the Babe Ruth Museum in Baltimore, which is one stop on the Bambino Trail, a six-night tour featuring the life and times of the legendary New York Yankees slugger.

Fans with an interest in collecting can enter the $3 billion market for sports memorabilia, which offers jerseys, balls, bats, photographs signed by athletes, and, in the case of at least one superstar, many more items. In 1997, a sale of Mickey Mantle's personal belongings at Leland's auction house in New York City netted $541,880. His passport sold for $9,200, his signed American Express Card for $7,175, and a lock of his hair for $6,900, almost ten times more than the preauction estimate of $700. Mantle's representatives could have made even more money, but they declined to sell many of the late slugger's belongings that were deemed too personal. Those included his bathrobe, prescription medicine bottles, and reading glasses. A second option for the consumption minded is official team merchandise. In addition to popular items like hats and jackets, there are a host of others available for purchase: ties, wastebaskets, mouse pads, duffel bags, earmuffs, comforters, calendars, shower curtains, shaving cream mugs, stuffed animals, telephones, flags, clocks, and rugs.

Why do so many people devote so much time and energy to following sports? British author George Orwell described sports as "war minus the shooting," and the emphasis on aggression and physical violence is clearly a factor in their vast popularity. A second factor is their ability to inspire uplift and hope. Earl Warren, the chief justice of the U.S. Supreme Court from 1953 to 1969, said that the front page of the newspaper reported failures, while the sports page reported accomplishments. In a world overflowing with self-doubt and broken dreams, the ongoing parade of athletic triumph is a source of optimism. But sports offers more than aggression, violence, and the chance for those who lead ordinary lives to experience joy at the achievements of others. In the course of a single contest, a full season, and a lifetime, sports fans can encounter comedy, tragedy, glamor, and high drama. They also can develop a kinship with people who share their devotion, a deep and durable bond that many of them cannot achieve readily in any other aspect of their lives. What effect does that deep devotion have on their spouses, families, careers, and communities? And what price is paid by individuals and by society when fans cross the line between devotion and derangement and become stalkers, arsonists, rioters, and murderers? . . .

The Lives of Sportsaholics

In his book *Not Now, Honey, I'm Watching the Game*, Kevin Quirk, a former sportswriter for the *Charlotte Observer* and correspondent for *Sports Illustrated*, profiles the lives of sportsaholics, broadly defined as people who live life through sports or for sports. Despite the book's humorous title, it is a serious attempt to gauge the negative effects of excessive devotion to sports. In an effort to determine the extent of the phenomenon, Quirk conducted a nationwide survey of sportsaholics and the women who love them. The results astonished him. He had touched a raw nerve, and a deluge of responses from tearful, frustrated women and proud, unapologetic men poured into his Charlottesville, Virginia, home by fax, letter, telephone, and e-mail.

Quirk uncovered a colorful gallery of sports-obsessed characters: one Pittsburgh Steelers fan who grew a stubbly beard in imitation of the team's quarterback Neil O'Donnell and another who dropped to his knees in tearful prayer in front of the television during a key playoff game. A University of Kentucky basketball fan who walks his dog during each game because it always seems to increase the team's lead. A man who watches every game with the same amount of change in his pocket—two quarters, one dime, two nickels, and one penny—to bring his team good luck, and another who once paced so nervously during games that he now has taken to hopping on one foot, causing friends to nickname him The Stork. For these men, a victory for their team creates excitement, giddiness, euphoria, and loud celebration; a defeat leads to despair, sullenness, anger, and an occasional outburst of violence.

Many sportsaholics expand their interest beyond the core activity of watching games. In Fantasy Leagues, a number of fans, usually between eight and sixteen, assemble to conduct a draft of a sport's players through which they assemble their own teams. In the week before the MLB season opens in April, groups of excited men toting clipboards and magazines can be observed holding their drafts in restaurants and bars everywhere. Identical gatherings occur in August before the NFL season and in October before the National Basketball Association (NBA) season. The performance of each fantasy team is then gauged by the statistics that the team's players compile in games actually played in real life. The fantasy player who com-

The Prevalence of Sports Gambling

The last Sunday in January has become the biggest day of the year for American bookmakers. Super Bowl Sunday has also become the nation's most popular unofficial holiday, a day for friends, football, food, and drink—and a time for placing a bet. During the last decade of the twentieth century, Americans wagered an estimated $3 billion on this one game alone. About $75 million was wagered per game in Nevada's sports books, enabling them to squeeze out profits ranging from $400,000 to $7.5 million, although they lost $500,000 on the 1995 game between San Diego and San Francisco when heavy money poured in on the 49ers in the hours before kickoff. But although the national media inevitably focuses on Nevada's Super Bowl betting, at least 95 percent of the money wagered on the game is handled by illegal bookies in the other forty-nine states; offshore "virtual" sports books available on the Internet are grabbing an increasing share of the action.

Richard O. Davies and Richard G. Abram, *Betting the Line: Sports Wagering in American Life*. Columbus: Ohio State University Press, 2001.

piles the best record by the end of the season is the champion. The champion usually wins a significant purse, made up of entry fees paid by each league member. In Fantasy Leagues, fans with strong statistical knowledge can become champions. They also can become fixated on the performance of individual players, a development that concerns some onlookers who believe fantasy owners lose interest in how real-life teams perform as a unit. That concern does not stop many athletes themselves from organizing Fantasy Leagues. During the 1997 NFL season, the most popular diversion in the New York Giants locker room was fantasy basketball, with fullback Charles Way serving as league commissioner.

On radio, sportsaholics can tune into sports talk stations such as WFAN "The Fan" in New York City; WTEM "The Team" in Washington, D.C.; and KTCK "The Ticket" in Dallas, Texas. Cheap shots, insults, put-downs, and macho bluster are the order of the day. The most popular hosts use brutal cynicism to denigrate teams, players, coaches, and even members of the listening audience who sometimes wait hours for a chance to talk on the air for thirty seconds or less. Al Morganti, a member of the sports crew at WIP in Philadelphia, says that when he comes to work each day, he checks his conscience at the door. There is no pretense of reporting facts; the shows traffic in opinions and rumors. "There's no accountability," says a staffer at Morganti's station. "It's dangerous, it's mean-spirited, it's almost a disgrace that it works."

The listeners, phone-in callers, and hosts of sports talk radio inhabit the same world, and through their love of sports they develop a perverse bond of mutual dependency that is tinged with affection, friendship, and even love. It is precisely this bond that alarms Quirk and the legions of women who responded to his survey. The love of sports can become so consuming that it corrodes all but the strongest unions between husband and wife. When a fan pours all of his emotion and energy into baseball, basketball, or football, there is little left for his wife, children, career, and community. That is a recipe for marital disaster. Quirk's first marriage ended in divorce, and he blames the failure on his own excessive sports-viewing habits.

How can a sportsaholic change? Quirk offers a number of strategies for mapping out a new game plan: rating the importance of each week's sports events and watching only those that are most critical, spending an hour with a wife or other partner for every hour spent watching sports, logging the amount of time spent with sports and then committing to a reduction. He does not recommend that anyone quit the habit completely. For serious fans reveling in what Quirk calls Sports Glut USA, that would be asking the impossible.

Crossing the Line

Some fans' hunger is not satisfied by watching games on television or indulging in other activities like listening to sports talk radio, playing in Fantasy Leagues, or collecting memorabilia or team merchandise. These fans, whether they act alone or in a group, twist their fixation with sports into something far darker that enters the realm of criminality.

Like other celebrities in the public spotlight, sports stars have been stalked by unstable fans. In 1949, a nineteen-year-old woman named Ruth Ann Steinhagen developed an infatuation with Philadelphia Phillies first baseman Eddie Waitkus. She invited him to her hotel room in Chicago when the Phillies were in town to play the Cubs. Once he was inside, she pointed a shotgun at his chest and pulled the trigger. Steinhagen then turned the gun on herself but could not summon the courage to take her own life. Waitkus was critically wounded, but he survived the attack and resumed his playing career. Steinhagen was committed to a mental hospital for three years. Her motive for the attack apparently was unrequited love. When she realized that a relationship with Waitkus was impossible, she tried to end both of their lives. Tainted love also was the motive of a forty-seven-year-old California man who relentlessly pursued Olympic figure skater Katarina Witt in 1992. He sent her nude photographs of himself and sexually explicit letters in an effort to kindle a romance. After being apprehended, he spent thirty-seven months in a mental hospital.

Some fans stalk athletes for reasons other than love. An Ohio man who described himself as a devout Christian was arrested in 1997 at the Chicago White Sox spring training camp in Sarasota, Florida. He was there to harass outspoken outfielder Albert Belle, just acquired by the White Sox in a trade with the Cleveland Indians. The man told police he was disgusted by Belle's belligerence and that Belle needed "to atone for his treatment of Cleveland fans." Another deranged man bolted onto the court at a tournament in Hamburg, Germany, in 1993 and stabbed tennis star Monica Seles in the back with a nine-inch knife. He wanted to injure Seles so that Steffi Graf, a fellow German, could regain the number one ranking in women's tennis. Maryland attorney Robin Feckler, nicknamed the Superheckler, has been a fixture at Washington Wizards' basketball games for many years. He is there to harass the team's opponents from his seat behind the visitors' bench.

There are also fans who simply use sports events as a springboard for vandalism. Writer Joe Queenan believes that "ugly antisocial behavior" is the norm for many New York Jets supporters, whom he calls "the worst fans in America." Jet fans routinely fight with each other, hurl batteries onto the playing field, and fling mounds of garbage into the concrete walkways that surround Giants Stadium, where the Jets play their home games. The most notorious incident occurred at a Monday night NFL game in 1988, when several fans ignited fires in the stands. The resulting mayhem led to fifteen arrests, five hospitalizations, fifty-six ejections from the stadium, and forty fistfights. At the same stadium in 1996, New York Giants fans attacked the visiting San Diego Chargers with a barrage of snowballs and iceballs. Charger equipment manager Sid Brooks was hit in the face and knocked unconscious. Among the fifteen people arrested was a retired police chief. "I'm concerned about the lack of personal responsibility people seem to feel when they come to a sports event," said Robert Mulcahy, head of the New Jersey Sports and Exposition Authority, which operates Giants Stadium. "There seems to be an increased sense that when you buy a ticket you have the right to behave any way you want." In 1997, when fighting and alcohol-induced rowdiness reached an unacceptable level at Philadelphia Eagles games, authorities set up a makeshift courtroom in a maintenance room in Veterans Stadium to dispense justice. On the first Sunday of the campaign, Judge Seamus P. McCaffrey fined seventeen fans and expelled them from the stadium. At least twenty teams have installed state-of-the-art cameras in their facilities to zero in on fans who start fights or throw projectiles from the stands. The systems cost about $100,000, an expense that more and more teams are willing to incur in their efforts to curb unacceptable behavior at their games.

The frequency and intensity of fan mayhem in the United States falls far short of what occurs in Great Britain. British soccer fans have a long history of bloodshed and destruction. Sixty-six people died in Scotland in 1971 when fans stampeded during a match at the home stadium of the Glasgow Rangers. On May 29, 1985, in Brussels, Belgium, violence erupted just before the English superpower Liverpool was scheduled to meet Juventus, an Italian team, in the finals of the European Cup tournament. After whipping themselves into a drunken frenzy before the match, the Liverpool supporters attacked the Juventus fans with knives, bottles, chains, and fence posts. Thirty-eight people died, and more than 250 were injured. After the tragedy, English soccer teams were barred from competing on the European continent for six years. In 1989, ninety-four died and 170 were injured at Hillsborough Stadium in Sheffield, England, when thousands of fans without tickets smashed through barricades to see a match between Liverpool and Nottingham Forest. . . .

Experts in the fields of criminology, psychology, and sociology have labored hard and long to determine the motives of the soccer hooligans. The critical elements the experts have identified are youth, maleness, working-class backgrounds, and a desire to protect territory or turf against encroachers. In the end, the words of one hooligan himself seem as apt an explanation as any: "Football is one tribe against another. We fight 'cos we like fighting."

The motives of the more passive breed of sports fanatics also have proved elusive. The key attractions are the unending drama of sports and the opportunity they offer to escape, at least temporarily, the burdens and mundanity of daily existence. For every wife who continues to shout, "Get a life!" to her spouse planted on the couch in front of the television set, there will be a husband who continues to reply, "This is my life, and I like it very much!"

Professional Athletes as Role Models

Sean Paige

Especially successful sports stars usually become celebrities in American society, and they are often regarded as heroes. However, as basketball star Charles Barkley famously pointed out in a 1995 Nike advertisement, not all pro athletes should be regarded as role models. In the late 1990s, a number of unsportsmanlike, sordid, and even criminal incidents involving sports figures once again raised the debate about whether athletes should be so highly regarded by general society. Sean Paige, who was an investigative reporter for *Insight on the News* magazine when he wrote the following article, explores the phenomenon and how fans are responding to it. He considers whether the bad behavior of some athletes is part of the nature of pro sports, or whether it is just another symptom of America's celebrity-obsessed culture.

THE ECONOMICS OF SPORTS ENTERTAINMENT have transformed many star athletes into multimillionaire prima donnas with little in common with—or use for—even their fans.

Often waiting in line overnight, crowds—sometimes hundreds of thousands strong—would surge into the stadium at first light, jostling for their places before the big game. Oblivious to the elements—slashing rain or scorching sun—spectators spent the day wildly cheering their favored team and col-

■

Sean Paige, "Sports Gladiators, Bread and Circuses," *Insight on the News*, vol. 14, August 3, 1998, pp. 8–12. Copyright © 1998 by News World Communications, Inc. Reproduced by permission.

ors to victory or defeat, with the most dramatic contests sometimes ending in sudden death or a street riot.

Bread and Circuses

But the Super Bowl or World Cup this was not. It was Constantinople, circa 500 A.D., under the Roman emperor Anastasius, and on this day the Green team came through in the clutch, British historian Edward Gibbon recounts, producing daggers and stones smuggled onto the field to murder 3,000 of the Blues. Although admittedly a bloody day for the Blues, who were to avenge this loss many times over during the reign of Justinian (a stalwart Blues backer), the slaughter represented a relatively mild afternoon at the city's colossal hippodrome, where the ferocity of the contests had been only slightly tamed by the Christian influence.

Imperial Rome had its gladiators, America has its gridiron greats. And just as Gibbon held up Rome's growing preoccupation with grotesque circuses as a barometer betraying a society's decay, the fall from grace of America's sports idols may be auguring something troubling about our own national soul.

Of course, Americans are not yet taking "bread and circuses"—government giveaways and sport spectaculars—to the extremes described by Gibbon in his famous *Decline and Fall of the Roman Empire*. Rather than feeding Christians to the lions, our Sunday-afternoon bloodlust more often is sated by pitting the Lions against the Saints, two National Football League teams seemingly caught in a Grail-like quest for a wild-card playoff spot.

Yet in Gibbon's account of the ancients we still can see eerie reflections of ourselves: cities staking their sense of identity and prestige on the games; public funds being plundered for ever more gaudy spectacles and grandiose stadiums; "idle multitudes" of citizens, "their minds agitated with hope and fear," devoting their lives to their beloved colors [as stated by Jennifer G. Hickey]; politicians being drawn into sports rivalries and issues; and a win at any cost used to excuse every excess of increasingly lawless gladiators.

"Every law, either human or divine, was trampled under foot, and as long as the party was successful, its deluded followers appeared careless of private distress or public calamity"

Gibbon writes. Before long the empire's "dissolute youth," taking their cues from the lawless gladiators, were caught up in the mayhem, the historian reports. And because "the laws were silent" in response, Gibbon laments, "the bonds of society relaxed."

The "relaxing" of societal discipline is something with which America, too, is wrestling, and our own elite athletes, once held up as heroes personifying strength, courage, fair play and other national virtues, often seem to be surfing the wave of chaos sweeping the country. Consider some of these instant replays—boxer Mike Tyson, a convicted rapist, biting a piece off the ear of Evander Holyfield; Golden State Warriors shooting guard Latrell Sprewell choking coach P.J. Carlesimo; Baltimore Orioles second baseman Roberto Alomar spitting in an umpire's face; Chicago Bulls forward Dennis Rodman kicking a spectator in the groin; and, yes, O.J. Simpson trying on the bloody glove. Who will say that in all of this we are not looking at our societal pathology writ large?

While the vast majority of our most celebrated athletes may be good citizens and worthy of emulation, increasingly the sports pages are filled with tales of criminality, greed, drug abuse, illegitimacy, spousal abuse and sexual license, with our pampered millionaire gladiators showing an impudent disregard for their actions and images. Into the admittedly idealized world America's sports heroes once inhabited come barbarian vandals, smashing the pedestals we put them on.

The Barkley Philosophy

From baseball's Babe Ruth evolved basketball's Charles Barkley, who stirred up controversy [in 1995] by officially repudiating his status as role model, suggesting that parents alone should bear that responsibility.

The sports world since has split into camps: those who ascribe to the Barkley philosophy, seeing his declaration of independence as a green light for licentiousness, and those who don't, such as former college-football star and now Republican Representative J.C. Watts of Oklahoma, who believes that an athlete's responsibilities as a citizen should temper his or her words and actions.

While Watts agrees with Barkley's point that parents matter most as role models for their children, his own experience as an athlete and politician testifies to the profound impact sports can have on character. "I agree with Charles when he says, 'Look, Mom and Dad can't put this responsibility on me,'" [says] Watts. "But I am also a firm believer that it is much more important to be a good citizen than it is to be a good athlete."

"Because of the stature and notoriety athletes have, they also have a responsibility, as citizens, to try to use whatever influence they have for positive things" Watts explains. Instead of giving him a license to indulge his personal appetites, being a star athlete "raised my awareness about my role as a citizen," says Watts, who is thankful that he always has had mentors and coaches who stressed responsibility and good citizenship.

Interestingly, Barkley made his "I-am-not-a-role-model" pronouncement in a television advertisement for Nike, which was using his name, image and reputation to promote its athletic wear—proving that in this era of the antihero one even can profit from thumbing one's nose at the people who put you on a pedestal. In fact, athletes have been trading on the outlaw image to sell products and heighten their celebrity—revealing a fundamental change in the way we think of them, according to some sociologists.

True, sport still is highly regarded in our society, celebrating virtues we revere such as competitiveness and courage. So much so that, "even though we see behavior to the contrary, we're willing to look the other way" according to University of Nevada, Las Vegas, sports sociologist Dr. Jim Frey. "We hold athletes up as role models, but we really don't expect them to be."

"We don't expect them to be value leaders, but we're not looking for that from them," Frey says of modern sports heroes. "We're really just valuing them for their skill. Nobody knows anything about Michael Jordan's values—he's worshipped because of his skill."

"We value achievement and would like to believe that people who are so exceptional in one area are exceptional in others," adds Michael Sachs, a sports psychologist at Temple University in Philadelphia. Many professional athletes would like to take Barkley's opt-out approach on the role-model issue, says Sachs, "but most athletes recognize that in actuality they do carry that burden."

After all, most of these athletic stars have been treated as something special from the time they could hit a home run or sink a jump shot from the top of the key. "These are the elite of the elite, and they've been pampered, they've been taken care of," says Sachs, creating and reinforcing their sense that they are exceptions to the rules.

Fallen Heroes

In our celebrity-addled culture, wherein every famous person's miscues are reported by around-the-clock media, it has become increasingly difficult to find a sports figure without flaws. "In order for someone to be a hero there has to be some sense of distance between them and us" says Frey. Without that distance, "we can't keep them on a pedestal," says Frey. In the past, "the media pretty much left private lives alone; now it's no longer sacred territory."

News stories [in the 1980s] that former San Diego Padres first baseman Steve Garvey, who seemed the perfect all-American role model, had cheated on his wife and sired a child out of wedlock inaugurated the open season on sports celebrities, some sports experts say. And the hunting has been excellent ever since, thanks in no small measure to the dissolute lifestyles so many professional athletes lead in a world of fame, riches and constant travel.

Revelations [in 1989] concerning baseball great Pete Rose's gambling habits delivered another shock to the sports world. Then basketball legend Magic Johnson announced that he had acquired the AIDS virus [1991], heavyweight boxing champion Tyson went to prison [1991], figure skater Tonya Harding took out a contract on rival Nancy Kerrigan [1994] and O.J. Simpson took the nation on that low-speed chase [1994].

Today few sports idols escape from a long career with their shining armor undented. The Mark McGwires, Cal Ripkens, Grant Hills, Emmett Smiths and Barry Sanderses are out there, of course, but their steady good citizenship often is overshadowed by ugly headlines about less-virtuous colleagues. As the venerable Green Bay Packers defensive lineman Reggie White discovered, when he ran afoul of the thought police by using complementary stereotypes during public remarks about race, even a model citizen-athlete can be just one slip of the tongue away from ignominy.

Meanwhile, in this gilded age of the antihero many seem to delight in puncturing the inflated reputations of past heroes. Thus, Ruth was a gluttonous, drunken womanizer, we now hear, and Ty Cobb an abject scoundrel.

It may be human nature to idealize as heroes sports figures from the past, but there is little evidence that there is less sportsmanship today than there was in some supposed golden age. "My sense is that, yes, there's some poor sportsmanship out there, but I would never say that it's worse today than it was 40 years ago," says Jay Coakley, a sports sociologist at the University of Colorado at Colorado Springs. "Babe Ruth was a hayseed, but that's not the way we want to remember him. We don't want to remember him coming to the ballpark hung over after he'd spent the night with another woman; we want to remember him pointing to the centerfield bleachers" to announce a homer for a sick kid.

We remember our sports heroes—all our heroes, in fact—for their virtues, says Coakley. "To keep some sense of sanity and an anchor in our lives, we remember some things better than others."

Are Fans Losing Interest?

Even as the economics of sports entertainment have transformed many of our star athletes into multimillionaire prima donnas who have little in common with the average American, those same economics may have begun to shut out and alienate lower- and middle-class fans upon whom the whole pyramid rests. "A lot of people are losing interest in [big-league sports] because they don't feel connected to it like they did in the past," explains Frey. And it's little wonder, when tickets are so expensive, the players so petulant, owners hold the fans hostage to win public financing for their stadiums and free agency has turned the roster of every ball club into a bus transfer for a list of passengers making brief stops between coaches on the road to the big bucks.

Television ratings have slumped 30 percent since 1987 for big-league baseball, 14 percent for basketball and 22 percent for football. And while plenty of cities still tie their slumping sense of identity to a pro team—and will bend over backward to lure a franchise away from other cities—a recent poll by the *Los Angeles Times* indicated that 59 percent of that city's residents didn't consider having a professional football team a matter of life or death.

Ironically, cold, cruel capitalism may be what is hurting big-league sports, which until relatively recently—when players became free agents, able to sell their services to the highest bidder—were government-assured monopolies in practice. "Leagues have traditionally been run in a socialist fashion, controlled by a cabal of owners who determined the rules of the game," protected from laws against oligopolous collusion by an antitrust exemption, explains Rick Burton, who teaches sports marketing at the University of Oregon's Warsaw Center, part of the Lundquist College of Business.

Courts ruled that players are not mere laborers after former St. Louis Cardinal Curt Flood petitioned the commissioner of major league baseball in 1969 to block his trade to another major-league club, Burton recounts. Flood liked St. Louis, had established a life and business there and "didn't want to be sold like livestock" Burton says. His petition eventually was denied, but Flood's refusal to be traded "was the start of the process whereby [players] started taking control of their destiny," launching the era of free agency.

While free agency has paid off handsomely for professional athletes—[in 1998] annual salaries average $1.3 million for baseball players, $1.2 million for hockey players, $2.6 million for basketball players, and $751,000 for football players—it also has given owners a handy justification to boost ticket prices, while the fans who pay those prices frequently lose track of who's on first.

"The players aren't doing anything wrong asking for as much money as they can. It's pure capitalism," says Burton. "But it's also driven up costs all around the game." Indeed, a fan cost index produced by Team Marketing Report indicates that the cost to take a family of four out to the ball game is $114.82—which isn't peanuts, or Cracker Jacks for that matter, but is a bargain compared to the other professional sports. For a National Basketball Association game, that same family might pay more than $214. To see some professional hockey, you're talking almost $230.

As a result of the soaring costs and ticket prices, major-league sports may have "become inefficient entertainment products, because the average person can no longer afford them," says Burton.

Others may just be disgusted. Just as not every ancient Roman embraced the games, evidence suggests that many Americans are turned off by what they see, or are finding better things to do with their time and money than live vicariously through the exploits of strangers. "We have a generation coming up that isn't as enamored of football, baseball and basketball as we were," UNLV's Frey says.

The sports consumers of tomorrow are the toddlers and preteens of today, whose athletic options and interests are incredibly diverse. And if sports owners and promoters don't remain in touch with the young consumers, many are likely to go the way of the leather helmet and wooden tennis racket.

A New Sports Landscape

"The sports market has to be more astute, because the niches are being drawn more narrowly," says Burton. "Today, the most powerful person in sports is the soccer mom" he [says], because in today's climate of fear, kids just don't go down to the field or sandlot to play anymore. They spend more of their time close to home, in the yard or driveway, playing video games, or in adult-supervised activities. Peewee football may be too violent for the tastes of some modern moms, for instance, and T-ball not egalitarian enough. Americans still love sports, "but we are on the front end of a wave of change," says Burton, that is best exemplified by so-called extreme sports: competitive skateboarding, street luge, snowboarding, mountain biking, trick biking, sky surfing, pro beach volleyball, beach hockey and in-line skating, to name just a few. Such sports even have their own cable network, ESPN2, and their own championship showcase, the X-Games.

The emergence of the professional female athlete also is a major force on the new American sports landscape, experts say. A law called Title IX, which has been interpreted to require universities to spend equally on male and female athletics, is revolutionizing collegiate sports and, by extension, women's professional sports.

While female athletes long have had a high profile in tennis, golf, figure skating, gymnastics and track and field, they now are making inroads into team sports formerly dominated by men. The NCAA women's basketball tournament has received unprecedented media coverage and there are two professional women's basketball leagues; a women's professional softball league is attracting fans in many markets; and professional women boxers are achieving name recognition among fight fans.

While female athletes have for the most part remained unsullied by the kinds of ugly headlines their male counterparts regularly earn (with the notable exception of skater Harding), the white-hot spotlight of media attention may turn up some blemishes.

An "end of the innocence" is coming, says Washington sports attorney and columnist Ellen Zavian, when professional female athletes will begin to receive the same level of public scrutiny as their male counterparts. "Women right now are in a perfect light," says Zavian, but "are not immune from the problems male athletes have, and we're really headed in that direction."

But female fans approach their sports heroes differently than men do, says Zavian, taking a more holistic approach. Women pick a heroine "not only because of what she did on the court," says Zavian, but "girls like to hear more about their personal sides and stories." Men, on the other hand, "just want to see the stats."

Perhaps the best news, given the fallen state of America's sports pantheon, is that "the impact of sports heroes on our people is probably overblown," says Coakley, echoing the sentiments of many sports sociologists. While the youngsters tend to relate to sports figures "because they're some of the only adults they've ever seen having fun with what they are doing," such heroes and heroines are not likely to be the determining influence on a child's life unless that child is being raised in a moral vacuum.

"We don't get these messages directly from athletes," says Coakley. "We get them from parents, coaches and friends who use athletes to make moral and character points." The lessons children may take from their big-league idols "is not an automatic transfer" according to Coakley. "The impact of what we see in sports depends upon the context in which we're living our lives."

In spite of all this, Americans still doggedly root for the home team and its heroes—which in itself says something telling about the state of our society. "The base of the word fan is fanatic, so there's not necessarily a logical basis" to the phenomenon, says Temple University's Sachs. But Americans are "all looking for some kind of community," Frey points out. "In a world where people move around and families often fall apart, sports may be the closest thing to community some people find."

FOR FURTHER RESEARCH

Books

David L. Andrews, ed., *Michael Jordan, Inc.: Corporate Sport, Media Culture, and Late Modern America*. Albany: State University of New York Press, 2001.
> Essays in this anthology discuss how Michael Jordan has influenced popular culture not just as an athlete but also as a black celebrity, an advertising spokesperson, and a global symbol of American culture.

David L. Andrews and Steven V. Jackson, eds., *Sports Stars: The Cultural Politics of Sporting Celebrity*. New York: Routledge, 2001.
> This anthology examines the cultural significance of Michael Jordan, Dennis Rodman, Andre Agassi, Tiger Woods, Venus Williams, Wayne Gretzky, and ten other pro athletes.

Aaron Baker and Todd Boyd, eds., *Out of Bounds: Sports, Media, and the Politics of Identity*. Bloomington: Indiana University Press, 1997.
> The nine essays in this anthology are divided into three chapters: "Sports and the Revision of Masculinity," "Sports, Race, and Representation," and "Hollywood Sports Films and Contested Identities."

Jeff Benedict, *Public Heroes, Private Felons: Athletes and Crimes Against Women*. Boston: Northeastern University Press, 1997.
> Benedict argues that the media too often ignore incidents in which athletes commit rape or domestic violence, and discusses how the culture of college and professional sports may encourage such behavior.

Todd Boyd and Kenneth L. Shropshire, eds., *Basketball Jones: America Above the Rim*. New York: New York University Press, 2000.
> Authors in this anthology examine many cultural aspects of basketball, including the game's association with black identity, the special privileges awarded to basketball stars, incivility in basketball, and women's participation in the sport.

Richard O. Davies, *America's Obsession: Sports and Society Since 1945*. New York: Harcourt Brace College, 1994.

Davies traces the history of pro sports from the end of World War II to the 1990s, with emphasis on how sports have impacted civil rights.

Richard O. Davies and Richard G. Abram, *Betting the Line: Sports Wagering in American Life*. Columbus: Ohio State University Press, 2001.

This book offers a comprehensive history of the illegal but widespread practice of sports gambling, from the infamous Black Sox scandal of 1919 to modern times.

Robert Elias, ed., *Baseball and the American Dream: Race, Class, Gender, and the National Pastime*. Armonk, NY: M.E. Sharpe, 2001.

The twenty-three essays in this anthology discuss race, ethnicity, gender, and class as they relate to baseball and traditional American values such as equality of opportunity and the rule of law.

Jon Entine, *Taboo: Why Black Athletes Dominate Sports and Why We're Afraid to Talk About It*. New York: Public Affairs, 2000.

In this controversial book, Entine examines the various proposed genetic and sociological explanations for the dominance of blacks in pro sports; he also offers his own theory that cultural conditions may have amplified some hereditary aspects of black athleticism.

John R. Gerdy, *Sports: The All-American Addiction*. Jackson: University of Mississippi Press, 2002.

The author argues that sports (especially amateur sports) have the potential to benefit society but that pro sports have become a negative influence on society due to their rampant commercialism and win-at-any-cost mentality.

Elliot J. Gorn and Warren Goldstein, *A Brief History of American Sports*. New York: Hill & Wang, 1993.

The authors present a comprehensive history of American sports, from colonial times to the rise of pro sports in the twentieth century.

John Hoberman, *Darwin's Athletes: How Sport Has Damaged Black America and Preserved the Myth of Race*. Boston: Houghton Mifflin, 1997.

Hoberman argues that society's fixation on black athletic achievement has a negative effect on race relations, black academic achievement, and white athletic achievement.

Richard E. Lapchick, *Smashing Barriers: Race and Sport in the New Millennium*. Lanham, MD: Madison Books, 2001.
Lapchick addresses the issue of discrimination in the sports world, highlighting in the final chapter some of the positive developments for women and minorities that have occurred since the early 1990s.

National Geographic, ed., *Baseball as America: Seeing Ourselves Through Our National Game*. Washington, DC: National Geographic, 2002.
Dozens of authors, ranging from poet and philosopher Walt Whitman to musician Paul Simon, have contributed stories and reflections about the significance of baseball to this photograph-filled volume.

Mariah Burton Nelson, *The Stronger Women Get, the More Men Love Football: Sexism and the American Culture of Sports*. New York: Harcourt Brace, 1994.
The author links male dominance in sports to male dominance and discrimination in society as a whole, and argues that high school, college, and pro sports should not be segregated along gender lines.

Dennis Perrin, *American Fan: Sports Mania and the Culture That Feeds It*. New York: Avon, 2000.
Perrin attacks what he feels are the most socially harmful aspects of pro sports culture: crass commercialism, violence, and fans that Perrin argues tend to be racist, homophobic, chauvinistic, and obnoxious.

Larry Platt, *New Jack Jocks: Rebels, Race, and the American Athlete*. Philadelphia: Temple University Press, 2002.
Through profiles of athletes such as Michael Jordan, Muhammad Ali, John McEnroe, and Mike Schmidt, the author discusses how sports have impacted Americans' attitudes toward race and gender.

S.W. Pope, ed., *The New American Sport History*. Urbana and Chicago: University of Illinois Press, 1997.
This anthology is intended as an overview of the critical study of sports history, with scholarly articles examining specific sports and time periods throughout the nineteenth and twentieth centuries.

Douglas T. Putnam, *Controversies of the Sports World*. Westport, CT: Greenwood Press, 1999.
Putnam examines sixteen controversies surrounding amateur and pro sports, including sports figures as role models, free agency,

sports gambling, publicly financed stadiums, violence in boxing, and the pressure some parents put on child athletes.

David Rowe, *Sport, Culture, and the Media: The Unruly Trinity.* Philadelphia: Open University Press, 1999.
This book examines the relationship between sports and the media, with chapters devoted to sports journalism, sports commentary, sports photography, and sports films.

Gary A. Sailes, ed., *African Americans in Sport: Contemporary Themes.* New Brunswick, NJ: Transaction Publishers, 1998.
The essays in this anthology examine sports from a black perspective, with essays focusing on the importance of sports to many black communities and the social effects of black dominance in pro sports.

Lissa Smith, ed., *Nike Is a Goddess: The History of Women's Sports.* New York: Atlantic Monthly Press, 1998.
This inspirational volume offers a sport-by-sport history of women's athletic achievements.

Jules Tygiel, *Past Time: Baseball as History.* New York: Oxford University Press, 2000.
Tygiel examines the cultural significance of baseball during such historic events as the Civil War, the depression, the civil rights era, and the early years of the Cold War.

Lawrence A. Wenner, ed., *MediaSport.* New York: Routledge, 1998.
The seventeen essays in this anthology critically examine the sports media, including topics ranging from the marketing of sports, sports journalism, and the sport media's portrayal of themes such as race, gender, and masculinity.

David K. Wiggins, *Glory Bound: Black Athletes in White America.* Syracuse, NY: Syracuse University Press, 1997.
The author provides eleven biographical sketches of black athletes and discusses how their individual experiences influenced and were influenced by the societies in which they lived.

Joel Zoss and John Bowman, *Diamonds in the Rough: The Untold History of Baseball.* New York: Contemporary Books, 1996.
Sampling the breadth of baseball's impact on popular culture, this volume examines not only the history of the game itself but also more unusual topics such as early newspaper coverage of the sport, baseball cards, and baseball fiction.

Websites

Center for the Study of Sport in Society. www.sportinsociety. org
> The center's philosophy is that sports are a reflection of society with all of its good points as well as its negative ones. It works to reform sports for the better through programs that teach student athletes important life skills.

National Coalition Against Violent Athletes. www.ncava.org
> The coalition was formed in 1997 in response to the growing number of violent crimes committed by athletes in all areas of the sports world. It believes that athletes should be held to the same standards and laws as the rest of society, and it works to educate the public on this issue.

Women's Sports Foundation. www.womenssportsfoundation. org
> The foundation helps educate the public by providing facts, statistics, and background data on sports-related issues for women and girls.

INDEX

Aaron, Hank, 124–25
ABC network, 42, 46
ABC Sports, 42–43
"ABC's Wide World of Sports," 43–44
Abram, Richard G., 166
Ackerman, Val, 123
Adgate, Brad, 52–53
advertising
  debunking racial stereotyping through, 94–95
  development of sports media and, 133
  extreme sports and, 51, 54
  role modeling for young girls and, 117–18
  Super Bowl Sunday and, 11, 46
affirmative action, 123
African American(s)
  academic vs. sports pursuits by, 95–96
  athletes
    attraction of white audience to, 100–101
    baseball and, 129
    basketball vs. baseball and, 68–69
    celebrity status of, in basketball, 67–68
    debunking racial stereotypes on, 94–95, 103
    decrease in, 121
    genetics and, 99
    media on, 100
    myths on athletic ability of, 101–103
    NFL quarterbacks and, 128–29
    as politically inactive, 98–100
    social value of, 97–98
    statistics on, 120
    tennis and, 127
    women and, 109–10
  baseball and, 35–36
  civil rights movement and, 25
  discrimination against, 21
  as golf fans, 128
  as tennis fans, 127–28
  at turn of twentieth century, 17
  unrealistic faith in sports by, 96–98
  white appreciation for culture of, 100–101
Ali, Muhammad, 25–27, 68, 95
All-American Girls Baseball League, 109
Alomar, Roberto, 173
Amateur Athletic Foundation (AAF), 75
Ameche, Alan, 39
American dream
  baseball and the pursuit of, 56–57
  melting pot and, 59–60

restoring baseball's, 62–64
Arledge, Roone, 42–45
Asians, 121
athletes
  acting by, 32
  African American. *See* African American(s), athletes
  basketball
    celebrity status of, 67–68
    male vs. female, 116
    viewer intimacy with, 65–66
    see also WNBA (Women's National Basketball Association)
  criminality of, 173
  entertainment value of, 146, 147
  female. *See* women
  flaws in, 175–76
  lure of, being part of a "big-time" sport, 148
  overblown impact of, on youth, 179–80
  past vs. present, 176
  responsibility for positive role modeling by, 173–75
  salaries of. *See* salaries
  sports television emphasizing pain and sacrifice of, 79–80
  stalked by fans, 168
  television's marketing of, 139–40

Babe Ruth Museum, 164
Baltimore Colts, 39
Banet-Weiser, Sarah, 111
Barkley, Charles, 72–73, 98, 173–75
baseball
  American melting pot and, 59–60
  athlete salaries in, 177
  at ballparks, 33–34
  vs. basketball, 66, 67
  as cerebral, 60
  computer technology and, 34–35
  as democracy in action, 57–58
  development of individual identity and, 58–59
  early popularity of, 29–31
  economic disparities in, 61–62
  on eve of World War II, 20
  Fantasy Leagues for, 163–64
  following World War II, 10
  labor difficulties, 35
  as a national pastime, 36–37
  participation decrease in, 53
  as promoting positive values, 60
  pursuit of American dream and, 56–57
  racial issues in, 35–36, 60–61, 68–69

186